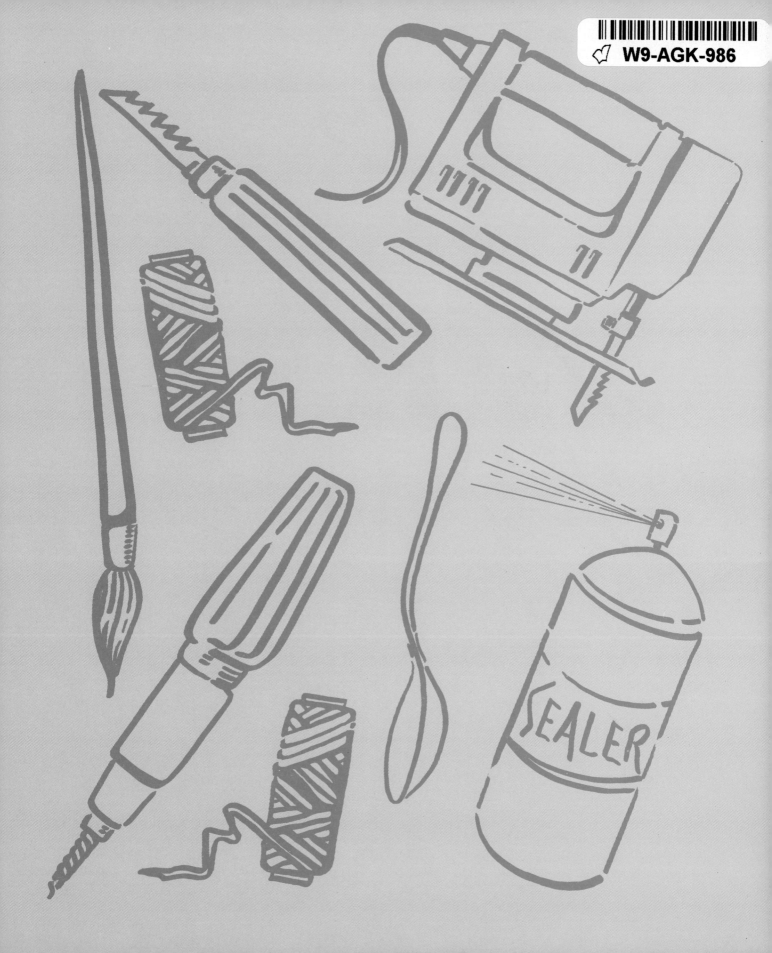

Gourd Crafts
for the first time®

Gourd Crafts
for the first time®

Marilynn Host

Sterling Publishing Co., Inc.
New York
A Sterling / Chapelle Book

Chapelle:

Owner: Jo Packham

Editor: Cathy Sexton

Staff: Areta Bingham, Kass Burchett, Ray Cornia, Marilyn Goff, Karla Haberstich, Holly Hollings-worth, Susan Jorgensen, Barbara Milburn, Karmen Quinney, Caroll Shreeve, Cindy Stoeckl, Kim Taylor, Sara Toliver, Desirée Wybrow

Photography: Kevin Dilley
                        for Hazen Imaging, Inc.
Photo Stylist: Jill Dahlberg

Gallery Photography: Various professional photographers unknown by name, unless indicated.

If you have any questions or comments or would like information on specialty products featured in this book, please contact:
Chapelle, Ltd., Inc.
P.O. Box 9252, Ogden, UT 84409
(801) 621-2777 • (801) 621-2788 Fax
e-mail: chapelle@chapelleltd.com
website: www.chapelleltd.com

Marilynn Host, OUT OF MY GOURDS
13450 Harding Ave., San Martin, CA 95046
(408) 686-1904

Library of Congress Cataloging-in-Publication Data Available

10 9 8 7 6 5 4 3 2

Published by Sterling Publishing Co., Inc.
387 Park Avenue South, New York, NY 10016
© 2002 by Marilynn Host
Distributed in Canada by Sterling Publishing
c/o Canadian Manda Group, One Atlantic Avenue, Suite 105
Toronto, Ontario, Canada M6K 3E7
Distributed in Australia by Capricorn Link (Australia) Pty. Ltd.
P.O. Box 704, Windsor, NSW 2756, Australia
Printed in China
All Rights Reserved

Sterling ISBN 0-8069-4423-4

This book is dedicated to all of my family—
young and old; near and far; present and passed.

Contents

Gourd Crafts for the first time

Introduction

For ages, gourds have been a part of cultures in North America, South America, Africa, and Asia. Though the information provided in this book will not explore the history of the gourd, it will create an atmosphere to learn more about them and the crafts that can be created from them. The intent of this book is to explore the many possibilities and techniques in creating one-of-a-kind gourd crafts.

Almost all parts of the gourd plant can be used—either for food or for utilitarian purposes. In the past, the most common use of gourds was as containers to transport and/or store wet and dry foods. In some countries, liquids were allowed to ferment in the gourds. The containers made from gourds were also used as storage containers for practical items such as medicines, seeds, herbs, oils, and other precious objects.

Gourds were also used as utensils for cooking. For example, the dipper gourd was commonly used as a ladle.

Musical instruments can be made from gourds. They include thumb pianos, drums, harps, banjos, and rattles.

In recent years, gourds have regained some of their popularity and have gained a place of acceptance in the craft world.

"Gourd Vessels" Dyed and airbrush-painted gourds embellished with waxed linen, dyed raffia, and beads. Approximately 8"x8"x8", 10"x10"x10", and 12"x12"x12".

How to use this book

For the beginning gourd crafter, *Gourd Crafts for the first time* supplies a basic understanding to creating wonderful pieces with gourds. The book guides you through the supplies you will need, basic techniques, interesting projects, and a beautiful gallery section. The book will get you started by teaching the basic skills involved in gourdwork and then let you explore an entire range of possibilities in finished projects. The first few techniques may take you some time to master, but in the end you will reap the benefits of beautiful gourdwork.

Section 1 supplies you with a list of the tools and supplies that are needed in order to complete the various techniques and projects in this book. This section also gives you a brief description of how these tools and supplies work.

Section 2 takes you through a series of basic techniques for learning gourd crafting. With each technique there will be a completed project. Some techniques are more difficult to master and will therefore require practice and patience on the part of the crafter.

Section 3 leads you through a series of projects in which the techniques that are learned in Section 2 are used in a more challenging way. Again, the projects will vary in difficulty.

Section 4, the Gallery, provides a visual treat of gourdwork by professional gourd artists. Their creations show the wide variety of artwork, imagination, and style that can be accomplished with practice and patience.

After you have finished the projects in this book, experiment further with the techniques you have learned. Do the same project on a differently shaped gourd, change colors, and create your own design.

Section 1: *gourd crafting basics*

What is a gourd?

A gourd is an inedible, hard-shelled fruit used for ornaments and implements. It is a member of the tendril-bearing vine family, which includes the cucumber, squash, and melon.

There are two basic types of gourds that you will be using for the projects in this book. They are the hard-shelled ornamental gourd and the soft-shelled ornamental gourd.

Within the two types, there are many different seed varieties. The seed variety determines the shape and size of the gourd. Canteen gourds are shaped like canteens, just as egg gourds, shown at right, are shaped like eggs.

The hard-shelled gourd is distinguished from the soft-shelled gourd by its shiny surface, yellowish tan color, and the thickness of its shell. The thickness of a good quality gourd is anywhere from $1/4"$ to $1"$, hence the name—hard-shelled. The hard-shelled gourd does not absorb water and is suitable for carving.

The soft-shelled gourd is distinguished from the hard-shelled gourd by its light color—light beige to white. In addition, the thickness of its shell is very thin—$1/8"$ or less. Because of this, it is easily broken. When immersed in water for a length of time, the shell will become soft and mushy.

An assortment of unwashed gourds.

12

All varieties of gourds have a growing season from approximately May to October and a drying period from two months to one year or more. This drying period is called the "curing stage." The curing process depends on the seed variety, the size of the gourd, and the climate conditions. During the curing stage, the gourds are considered to be in a fragile state. If they are scratched or bruised, the gourds may rot rather than harden. Keep in mind that all of the gourds needed for the projects in this book must be selected from last year's crop.

A gourd will last practically forever if properly cared for and preserved. Any gourd, whether hard-shelled or soft-shelled, will deteriorate and disintegrate if exposed to the elements. Birdhouses made for the outdoors, even though they are sealed, will probably last only one season.

Unwashed bottle gourd, approximately 10"x10"x12".

An assortment of washed gourds.

How many gourd varieties are there?

When choosing the variety of gourd you will be using, choose gourds that have their stems still attached. The stems are used in many cases to hang the gourds until dyes, polishes, and/or paints dry. Stems are also incorporated into several project designs such as arms on the Snowman on page 56, a nose on the Gourd Critter on page 64, and can be substituted for the twig perch on the Bird-house on page 70.

Stems incorporated for arms in the snowman design.

Bottle Gourds

The bottle gourd category includes several gourd varieties, including the common "bottle" gourd, the pear-shaped or Martin House gourd, and the mini hard-shelled gourd. All of these gourds are characterized by having a body, a neck, and a bulb-like head on top. For the most part, they will have a flat bottom.

They come in a variety of sizes—anywhere from 3" in diameter to approximately 14" in diameter. However, there is a miniature variety of these gourds. These gourds are used primarily for making vessels, birdhouses, and birdfeeders. The miniature variety is used to make holiday ornaments. The bottle gourds used in the projects in this book are Chinese bottle gourds.

Bowl Gourds

Familiar names in the bowl gourd variety include the tobacco box, the apple, the canteen, the bushel basket, the cannonball, and the basketball. These gourds are round—they have no necks and no heads.

The tobacco box, canteen, and bushel basket gourds will generally have a flat bottom, whereas the cannonball and basketball gourds will be almost totally round and have a small nipple at the stem end. Cannonball and basketball gourds are very similar in shape except for the fact that the basketball gourd is larger.

Bowl gourds come in a variety of sizes measuring from 4" in diameter to 20" in diameter. They are used primarily for making bowls, containers with lids, baskets, drums, and masks.

Dipper Gourds

Dipper gourds are characterized by a round bulb-like bottom and a long neck. The necks can be curved or straight—depending on how they are grown. For example, if grown on trellises, the necks can grow very straight and long, oftentimes up to 6' in length. If grown on the ground, the necks will become curved or curled. The bodies will range in size from 4" to 8" in diameter.

Dipper gourds are used to make ladles and rattles.

Ornamental Gourds

This group of gourds includes the egg, the wartie, the crown of thorns, and a variety of other shapes. Some people refer to the other shapes as apples, oranges, and pears. These gourds are soft-shelled and are fairly small in size—usually no larger than approximately 4" in diameter.

They are used primarily for crafting ornaments and decorative objects.

Snake Gourds

In the snake gourd variety, you will find the snake, the club, and the banana gourds. These gourds are characterized by their long bodies. They will generally have a flat side because of how they grew in the field.

Though the length of the snake or club gourds can reach 6', they do not get much larger than approximately 8" in diameter. The banana gourd is a smaller version.

The snake and club gourds are used to make trough-like containers. The banana gourd is used to make Santas, ornaments, and decorative fruits.

How do I grow and harvest my own gourds?

Growing gourds is very similar to growing any member of the squash family. It actually takes little effort to produce a nice crop of interesting gourds.

Choosing which varieties of gourds you want to grow will be the first step. Gourds are hybrids. Each seed within a gourd has been fertilized by a different pollen grain, therefore it is impossible to calculate exactly what the gourd will be like unless special care has been taken in the pollination of the gourd plant for past generations. Specialty seed companies and nurseries should be able to provide seeds that will produce the particular size and shape of gourds you desire.

When you are ready to plant the seeds, make certain you have planned your garden so that single varieties of gourds are spaced far from other varieties. This will eliminate the possibility of cross-pollination.

Unwashed bottle gourd, approximately 8"x8"x12".

You will need to start with fertilized soil, water regularly, and make certain the gourd plants get plenty of sunshine. Plant the seeds approximately 1½" deep, either in rows or in mounds, spaced approximately eight feet apart. They can also be planted in containers. You will want to enrich the soil occasionally throughout the growing season.

It will take approximately 100 days for the gourds to reach maturity, so they can be harvested. While growing, the gourds are usually white to light green in color. Toward the end of the season, the gourds' growing process slows and skin, called the epidermis, starts to form on the outside of the gourds.

After the first frost, the gourd vines start to die and the gourds begin to dry. At this point the gourds will have their shells, but they won't be as hard as they will get. At the same time, the color starts to change to yellowish tan. As the gourds continue to dry, the shells become harder and mold will begin to attack their surfaces.

If you are planning to save seeds from the gourds you have grown, make certain the gourds have not frozen, as frozen seeds will not germinate. Seeds can be stored in glass or plastic containers for up to four years.

When the stems of the gourds appear brown and the tendrils next to the gourds are dry, the fully mature gourds can be picked. When picking, try to leave a portion of the stem attached to the gourd. If colored ornamental gourds are left on the vine, the colors will fade in the sunlight. After the mature gourds have been picked, the vine and the remaining gourds will continue to grow.

Many gardeners recommend leaving the gourds on the vine to dry. If you live in a mild, dry climate you can do this. If you live in a colder climate, this is not possible; if the gourds become wet or frozen, the shell will begin to rot. When left in the field to dry, the gourds must be turned approximately once a week to ensure even drying and to prevent the gourds from flattening on one side. This is especially important when growing gourds 12" in diameter and larger.

Unwashed bushel basket gourd, approximately 10"x10"x10".

Unwashed canteen gourd, approximately 10"x10"x6".

19

How do I preserve a gourd?

The preservation of gourds will depend on where the gourds are grown. For example, if you live in the warmer and drier climates, not high in elevation, you can leave the gourds to dry in the field. If you live in the northern climates or where there are severe winters, you will need to bring the gourds into a barn or cellar to protect them from freezing conditions. In any case, the drying, or "curing," stage will take until the following spring. Gourds left to winter in the field will be covered with dirt and mold. They can be washed off when the gourd is dry.

Depending on the size of the gourd, it is sometimes difficult to tell when it is thoroughly dry. With a little bit of experience one will get a feel for dryness. Usually the seeds will rattle or they will stay together in a round ball and "thunk" when you shake the gourd. If you have a gourd that thunks, it can create a problem for cleaning. The ball of seeds on the inside is very hard and takes up most of the space. If the cut opening of the gourd is small, it will be difficult to break that seed ball apart and clean the inside of the gourd.

In any case, a dried gourd can last forever in a controlled environment. Direct sun, wind, and rain will deteriorate the gourd's shell. Oftentimes, gourds are washed and left in their natural uncut state.

Unwashed crown of thorns gourds, approximately 4"x4"x4".

"Crown of Thorns" An assortment of leather-dyed and airbrush-painted Crown of Thorns. Approximately 4" in diameter.

20

How do I repair a natural imperfection on a gourd?

One can spend a lot of time looking for the "perfect" gourd because natural imperfections are common.

First of all, the mold that has been on the outside of the gourd can leave a dark brown stain. It is permanent, so it is best to incorporate it into your design as shown in the photo on page 22. These natural markings can add depth to the surface, especially if you use the transparent coloring techniques, such as using leather dye, Ukrainian egg dye, or wax shoe polish.

One can also find imperfections like insect holes or animal nibbles. Deer like to do this, and can sometimes take a nice-sized bite from the gourd. Again, use this as part of your design. To try and patch these types of imperfections makes the flaw more obvious.

Insect holes, if they aren't too large, can be repaired with wood patch. Make certain to purchase a type that is water-soluble and will receive dye or paint. Any excess can be removed with a damp cloth.

Close-up photo of gourd with insect holes.

Washed bottle gourd with deer bite at the bottom.

How do I repair a broken gourd?

Generally I advise people to be cautious about spending too much time on repairing a broken gourd. In many cases the mend does not work. But, if you have a gourd that is near and dear to your heart, there are a few things that can be done.

To repair a crack, pull the gourd slightly apart and apply a small amount of glue. Woodworkers glue works best because it is stronger and sets up faster. Press the sides together, wipe off the excess glue, and tape the sides together with masking tape. Allow the glue to dry thoroughly.

For larger cracks, I have found that pressing papier-maché pulp into the crack will work. However, I have only done this on the inside and the bottom of a large gourd. This repair technique would work well if the gourd is going to be découpaged, as with the Victorian Gourd on page 51 and the Handmade-paper-covered Vessel on page 80.

Broken or cracked gourds are best used as scrap. Pieces can be attached together, as with the Snowman on page 56, or used to make Jewelry as shown on page 89. In any case, broken or cracked gourds can always be used to practice any of the techniques presented in *Gourd Crafts for the first time.*

Washed snake gourd patched with wood filler.

Gourd with imperfections incorporated into the design.

What precautions should I take when working with gourds?

Common sense is the key when working with gourds. Keep the following safety tips in mind:

• Always do the washing and cutting outdoors to allow for proper ventilation.

• Place the gourd to be cut on a nonslip surface such as a rubber mat.

• You may need to brace the gourd against a wooden form to hold it steady.

• Always hold the gourd firmly when cutting.

• Always wear a dust mask. This is especially important for people who are allergic to dust and fixed molds.

• Work downwind or have a fan blowing behind you. This causes the gourd dust to blow away from you.

• Wash your hands often when working with gourds. Some people's skin will have an allergic reaction to the molds.

• Spiders like to live inside cut gourds. If a gourd has been sitting around for awhile, shake it upside down before putting your hand inside.

• If you are planning to use your cut gourd as a bowl, water vessel, or other container to hold food products, do not paint the inside with spray paint or other paints or sealers. Leave them in their natural state.

Gourd birdfeeder with carved design and drilled holes; twisted-twine hanger.

What washing supplies do I need?

1 Bucket

The bucket will be the container used for washing the gourd. It can be metal or plastic, but must be large enough to accommodate the gourd you are using. Galvanized metal buckets and/or tubs can be purchased at hardware stores and are available in a number of sizes. Plastic containers can be purchased at most local department stores and are available in a wide variety of shapes and sizes. For larger gourds, plastic containers are recommended because of their light weight. In addition, plastic containers with lids make excellent storage containers for gourds.

2 Dishwashing Detergent

A mild dishwashing detergent added to hot water in the bucket aids in the cleaning of the gourd.

3 Household Bleach

A few drops of household bleach in a bucket of sudsy water is excellent for sanitizing the surface of the gourd to prepare it for the project. Additionally, it will guard against the reappearance of mold on the gourd.

4 Paring Knife

A paring knife is used for scraping stubborn areas from the outside of the gourd.

5 Scrubbing Pads

Scrubbing pads are used to remove the thin skin from the gourd during the cleaning process. Several varieties are available, such as copper and nylon.

Tip:

Set up your washing and cutting supplies outdoors because crafting with gourds can be messy. This is especially important when working with larger gourds.

How do I clean the outside of a gourd?

1. Fill a bucket with hot water. Add a few drops of dishwashing detergent and a few drops of household bleach.

Note: The gourd will float. Turn it several times to make certain all areas get wet.

2. Using a scrubbing pad, scrub the gourd to remove the dirt, mold, and thin outer layer of skin as shown below.

Note: When clean, the gourd will have a nice tan color. Mold on the surface of the gourd will sometimes leave a permanent dark brown discoloration. There is nothing you can do about it if you want to keep the gourd in its natural state. Use this to your advantage.

3. If the gourd has a "white film" on the surface, all of the debris has not been removed. To remove the stubborn skin, soak the gourd in the bucket of hot soapy water. Using a paring knife, scrape away the remaining skin as shown below.

4. Allow the gourd to dry thoroughly.

Note: Avoid placing the gourd in direct sunlight to dry. This can cause large gourds to crack.

What cutting and drilling tools do I need?

1 Electric Drill and Drill Bits

An electric drill will be used in most of the projects. It does not need to be large or powerful. In fact, mini craft drills with less power are actually more practical. The drill bits should be small as well—1/4" and under.

2 Electric Jigsaw

An electric hand-held jigsaw will also be used in most of the projects. Again, the jigsaw does not need to be very powerful.

3 Serrated Craft Knife

A small serrated craft knife is used to begin any cut in the gourd. Replaceable serrated blades may be purchased at a local hardware store.

4 Spoons

Old spoons are used to scrape and remove the majority of the "pulp" from the inside of the gourd. This prepares the gourd for the wire-brush cleaning.

5 Wire Brush on Extended Drill Shaft

A small round wire brush is used on a drill shaft extension to clean the inside of the gourd. Wire brushes are available in several sizes. When cleaning larger gourds, a larger wire brush is preferred.

What paintbrushes do I need?

1   China-bristle Paintbrush

A china-bristle paintbrush is used to apply a large amount of painting medium onto the surface of the gourd in a short amount of time. It also can be used to apply leather dye and/or varnish.

2   Soft-bristled Paintbrushes

These paintbrushes are used to do the detail and decorative work on the gourd's surface. They come in flat and round styles and are available in a wide variety of sizes.

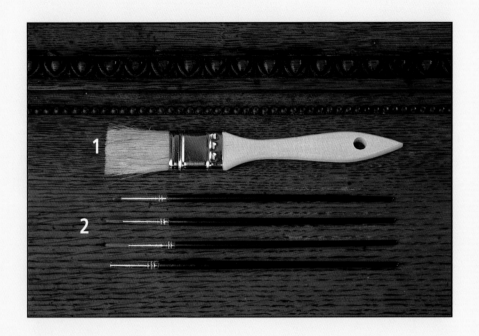

What sponges do I need?

1   Natural Sea Sponge

The natural sea sponge is used with the sponge-painting technique. It will give a nice mottled look to the gourd's surface. Keep in mind that if it is too large for the project you are working on, it can be easily cut into small sections.

2   Synthetic Sponge

This type of sponge is basically used for cleaning up. It can also be cut into small sections that can be used as stamps for painting.

3   Sponge Dauber

A sponge dauber is also known as a sponge pouncer. It is a small wooden stick with a sponge attached to one end. It is an applicator used to paint repeated decorative marks of the same size. The projects in this book use ¹/₄" or ¹/₂" sponge daubers.

27

What general supplies do I need?

1 Canvas Needles

Canvas needles are needed to stitch raffia around the cut edges of the gourds. They are available in various sizes. You will need one with an eye large enough to easily allow waxed linen to pass through.

2 Craft Sticks

Craft sticks are useful tools for stirring egg dyes. They also can be used as testing sticks to determine the intensity of the dye color. In addition, they can be used to apply patches to holes in the gourd's surface.

3 Disposable Gloves

Disposable gloves are recommended to protect your skin from the waxes and dyes when coloring any gourd.

4 Dust Mask

A dust mask is necessary to protect your lungs from the minute dust particles that come from the inside of a dried gourd. It should also be worn when you are spray painting.

5 Hot-glue Gun and Glue Sticks

In some instances, hot glue can be used to attach embellishments to the gourd.

6 Marking Pens

Marking pens are useful when outlining decorative areas. They are also useful in drawing designs on the gourd's surface. Any color can be used, but black seems to be the best choice.

7 Masking Tape

Masking tape is used to mask off a design area. It is also used to hold a gourd together when making a repair.

8 Needle-nosed Pliers

These pliers are used to snap off the gourd stems.

9 Pencil

A pencil is used in almost all projects to either mark a cutting line or to draw a design.

10 Rags

Rags are used for cleaning up. They are also helpful to remove excess egg and/or leather dyes from the gourd's surface.

11 Sandpaper

Fine-grit sandpaper is used to sand the gourd's surface after the stem has been removed. It is also used to smooth cut edges and drilled holes.

12 Scissors

A good pair of sharp scissors is a common basic tool that will be used often.

13 Tape Measure (not shown)

A fabric tape measure is used in almost all of the projects for general measurements such as lengths or circumferences.

14 White Craft Glue

White craft glue is used for attaching embellishments to the gourd. Keep in mind that craft glue is water-soluble; therefore, it should not be used on a gourd that will be displayed outdoors.

15 Wood File

A wood file is used to even and smooth the cut edges of the gourd.

What coloring agents do I need?

3 Spray Paint

For the most part, spray paints are semitransparent. However, some of the colors are more opaque than others. They are available in a wide array of colors and are relatively easy to use. Metallic copper, gold, and silver spray paints add a nice accent to any holiday item.

4 Ukrainian Egg Dye (not shown)

Ukrainian egg dyes are water-based and produce an intense and vivid transparent color. They are absorbed best on soft-shelled ornamental gourds.

1 Acrylic Paints

Water-based acrylic paints render a flat opaque color; therefore, you will not be able to see through to the surface of the gourd once it has been painted. They are available in a wide array of colors, including metallics, and are easy to use.

2 Leather Dye

Leather dyes are alcohol-based and produce an intense and vivid transparent color. They are a little difficult to use because they are fluid and tend to run easily. With practice, however, they will work well on any gourd's surface.

5 Wax Shoe Polish

Wax shoe polish gives a soft subtle color and the application is easily controlled. It produces a semiopaque appearance and comes in several colors. Colored waxes might have different tinting effects, depending on the porosity of the gourd. After its application, it can be buffed to a nice sheen.

What sealing agents do I need?

1 Acrylic Sealer

Clear acrylic spray sealer is used to seal the surface of the gourd and to protect it from moisture, dust, and dirt. It is used most often among sealers and is available in a gloss or a matte finish.

2 Floor Wax

Waxes in liquid form come in a variety of hardnesses, but the floor variety is best suited for the gourd. Floor wax gives a nice natural finish to the gourd's surface.

3 Ultraviolet-resistant Sealer

Ultraviolet-resistant spray sealer is also a good choice for sealing the surface of the gourd, but is available only in a gloss finish. This type of sealer will help protect the gourd's color from fading due to sunlight.

4 Varnish

Water-based varnish is recommended. It is easy to brush on and it cleans up easily with soap and water. It dries quickly to a clear, hard finish and is available in gloss, semigloss, and matte finishes. Spray varnish is also available.

What embellishments can I use?

1   Amulets/Beads

Amulets and beads may already be in your collection of decorative items to use. A variety of sizes is helpful.

2   Feathers

If you use feathers, make certain they are purchased in a craft store to assure they will be sterile and have no danger of insect infestation.

3   Charms (not shown)

Charms are available in a number of shapes and sizes. In addition, they are usually available in gold-tone and in silver-tone.

4   Leather Cord (not shown)

Leather cord can be used to decorate gourds or to attach ornaments. It is available in several colors.

5   Natural Pods

Natural pods can be collected from the outdoors or purchased from flower marts.

6   Raffia

Raffia is commonly used to decorate the cut edge of a gourd bowl. The most prominent color is natural, but raffia is available in several other colors. Raffias will vary in

texture; some are thin and stiff, while others are wide and soft.

7   Ribbon

Ribbon comes in a wide range of widths, textures, and colors. It can be used to decorate gourds or to hang ornaments.

8   Waxed Linen

Waxed linen comes in a variety of colors and is easy to work with because it will stick to itself. It is available in 3- and 4-ply. It is used when wrapping the gourd with raffia.

Large gourd features a lizard design stenciled onto the surface that has been dyed with leather dyes; embellished with leather cord, small feathers, and assorted beads.

Section 2:
basic techniques

How do I cut open, then clean the inside of a gourd?

Once your gourd has been thoroughly washed, the excess skin removed, and it has been allowed to dry, it can be cut. Next, the pulp is removed and the inside of the gourd must be cleaned.

Basic Bowl

Here's How:

Preparing the Gourd

1. Refer to How do I clean the outside of a gourd? on page 25. Scrub the gourd.

Cutting the Gourd Open

1. Using a pencil, mark the cutting line around the center of the gourd as shown below.

2. Wearing a dust mask and using an electric drill with a 1/16" drill bit, drill three holes into the gourd, positioned in a row on the cutting line as shown at right.

3. Using a serrated craft knife, push the blade into the gourd at the drilled holes as shown below, to make a cut long enough to accommodate the jigsaw blade.

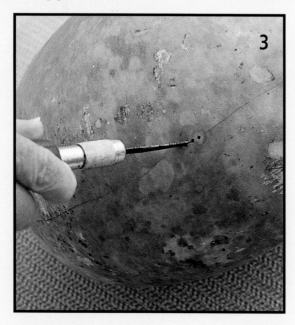

4. Using an electric jigsaw, continue the cut as shown below. Cut the gourd into two halves. Discard the half with the stem attached.

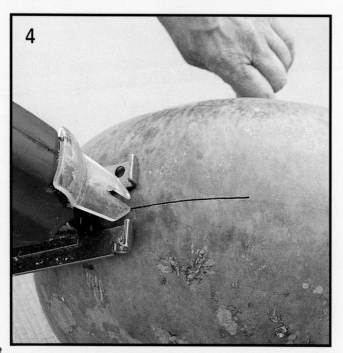

Cutting Tip: When cutting into a seed ball, the jigsaw can sometimes get stuck and cause the gourd to jump around while cutting. This is not a safe situation. To correct this, fill the gourd with water and let it soak for a day or two to soften the seed ball. Empty the water from the gourd and break the softened ball apart with a large screwdriver. Then allow the inside to dry—this could take a while. Once the inside is dry, it can be cleaned.

Cleaning the Inside of the Gourd

1. The inside of the gourd is filled with seeds, dried pulp, and gourd dust. Wearing a dust mask, shake out as much of the inside matter as possible.

2. Pull out as much of the remaining inside matter as you can with your hand as shown below.

Note: If the cut opening, or mouth, of the gourd is too small for your hand to fit into, continue on with Step 4 in first column on page 39.

3. Using a spoon, scrape away the remainder of the inside matter.

4. If the inside matter is persistent, a wire brush on the end of an electric drill must be used. Holding the bowl securely on a nonslip steady surface, begin the wire-brush cleaning as shown below.

Note: Sometimes mold will seep through to the inside of a gourd and permanently stain it. These imperfections cannot be removed. Enjoy them!

5. Using a wood file, file the cut edge as shown below to make it even.

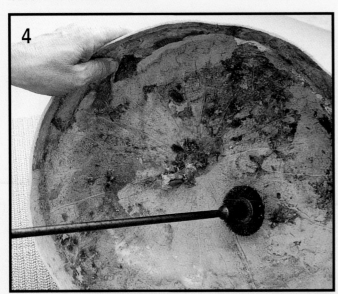

Finishing the Bowl

1. Using a $3/16$" drill bit, drill two holes parallel to the top edge, approximately $3/4$" down and $1^1/_2$" apart.

2. Wash the inside of the bowl in a bucket of hot soapy water. Rinse thoroughly with clean water, making certain that only a minimal amount of gourd dust floats on the surface. Allow the bowl to dry thoroughly on both the inside and the outside.

3. Using a china-bristle paintbrush, apply floor wax over the outside surface as shown below.

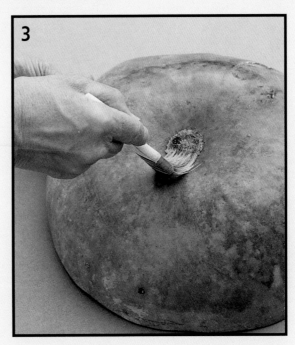

4. Push the leather cord through the two holes from the outside and tie a knot at each end on the inside of the bowl.

2
technique

What You Will Need:

- Tools and supplies,
  see pages 24–32
- Bottle gourd
- Spray paint, black
- Leather dye, dark red
- Acrylic sealer
- Suede, beige, 2" wide
- Decorative beads

How do I color the outside of a gourd with leather dye?

Leather dye is very fluid and has a tendency to run. To prevent unwanted messes, take care to not oversaturate the applicator. Work as quickly as possible to get a nice even coat of dye. As the dye dries, the coloring on the gourd's entire surface will be consistent.

Decorative Vase

Here's How:

Preparing the Gourd

1. Refer to How do I clean the outside of a gourd? on page 25. Scrub the gourd.

2. Refer to Technique 1: Cutting the Gourd Open on pages 37–38. Cut only the top off the gourd. Discard the top.

3. Refer to Technique 1: Cleaning the Inside of the Gourd on pages 38–39. Clean the inside of the gourd.

4. Wearing a dust mask and disposable gloves, aim the can of spray paint into the opening of the gourd. Apply an even coat to the inside of the gourd. Allow the spray paint to dry thoroughly.

Note: Several light coats are better than one heavy coat.

Coloring the Outside of the Gourd

1. Wearing disposable gloves and using the leather dye applicator, apply leather dye to the outside of the gourd. Start at the bottom and work toward the top as shown at right, turning the gourd upright when the bottom is covered. Cover the entire gourd.

2. Wait approximately 10 minutes, then using a clean rag, wipe off any excess dye. Allow the dye to dry thoroughly. This will take approximately two hours.

Finishing the Vase

1. Spray the vase with an acrylic sealer. Allow the sealer to dry thoroughly.

2. Using a hot-glue gun and glue sticks, apply a line of hot glue parallel to the top edge, approximately $1/4$" down and $3/4$" long.

3. Immediately wrap the suede around the top outside edge, leaving enough to go over the top edge and down the inside approximately $1/4$".

4. Repeat Steps 2 and 3 above, until the entire top edge of the vase is wrapped with suede.

5. Using scissors, trim the remaining end of the suede to snugly fit against the beginning edge.

6. Fold the suede over the top edge and hot-glue in place on the inside of the vase.

7. Using a pencil, mark the front center of the vase at the top.

8. Using a $3/32$" drill bit, drill a hole at the center mark through the suede and the gourd.

9. Thread a length of waxed linen through the eye of a needle. Double the length and knot the ends together.

10. Push the threaded needle from the inside of the vase through to the outside. Thread the large bead onto the waxed linen and tie a knot at the bottom of the bead. Cut the waxed linen at the needle, leaving two hanging lengths.

11. Thread the small beads onto each hanging length and tie a knot at each end.

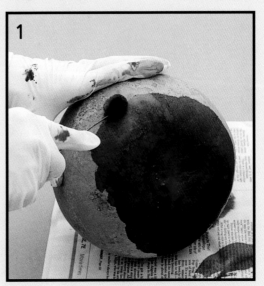

3
technique

What You Will Need:

- Tools and supplies, see pages 24–32
- Egg gourds
- Buckets
- Ukrainian egg dyes: gold, green, red
- Vinegar
- Terra-cotta pot
- Ultraviolet-resistant sealer
- Pony beads, gold
- Ribbons, 1/8"-wide, 8"
- Fine-tipped permanent marker, metallic gold
- Wide-tipped permanent marker, metallic gold

How do I color the outside of a gourd with Ukrainian egg dye?

Ukrainian egg dye works great on egg gourds because their soft shells absorb the dye. The dye color is a rich transparent jewel tone that contrasts with the metallic markers.

Ornaments

Here's How:

Preparing the Gourds

1. Refer to How do I clean the outside of a gourd? on page 25. Scrub the gourds.

Coloring the Outside of the Gourds

1. Prepare the egg dyes, following the instructions on the dye packets. Use a separate bucket for each dye color.

2. Place the gourds in the dyes as shown below.

3. Because the gourds will float, place a terracotta planter on top of them as shown below. The weight of the planter will immerse them. Soak the gourds in the dyes for 15 minutes.

4. Wearing disposable gloves, remove the gourds from the dyes and hang them by their stems to dry. Allow the dye to dry thoroughly.

Note: If the gourds do not have stems, place them on several sheets of newspaper to dry.

Finishing the Ornaments

1. Spray the ornaments with an ultraviolet-resistant sealer. Allow the sealer to dry thoroughly.

2. Using needle-nosed pliers, remove the stems as shown below.

Note: If a stem does not "snap off" cleanly, it must be sanded with sandpaper until smooth.

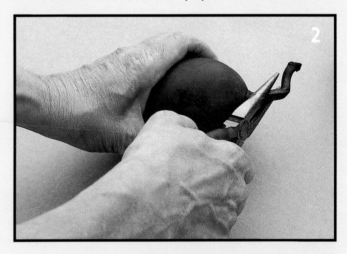

3. To make each ornament hanger, double one length of ribbon and place both ends through a pony bead. Using a hot-glue gun and glue sticks, place a small amount of hot glue on the ribbon ends and pull them back through until they are flush with the bottom edge of the bead. Repeat for each additional hanger.

4. Attach the bead on each hanger to the tops of the ornaments with hot glue where the gourd stems were removed.

5. Using a wide-tipped marker, draw designs on the ornaments. Using a fine-tipped marker, accentuate the designs.

How do I color the outside of a gourd with spray paint?

Coloring gourds with spray paint is fast and easy since the paint dries almost immediately. The jewel-toned colors will be semitransparent, whereas other colors will be opaque.

What You Will Need:

- Tools and supplies, see pages 24–32
- Apple gourds (2)
- Spray paints: gold, green, red
- Acrylic sealer
- Acrylic paint, brown
- Wire screen, 6"-square
- Wire cutters

Decorative Apples

Here's How:

Preparing the Gourds

1. Refer to How do I clean the outside of a gourd? on page 25. Scrub the gourds.

Coloring the Outside of the Gourds

1. Wearing a dust mask and disposable gloves, hold each gourd by its stem. Spray-paint one with green and one with red. Apply a light, even coat and hang them by their stems to dry. Allow the spray paint to dry thoroughly.

2. Repeat Step 1 above.

Note: Several light coats are better than one heavy coat.

Finishing the Apples

1. Using a soft-bristled paint-brush, paint the stems with brown acrylic paint. Allow the paint to dry thoroughly.

2. Spray the apples with an acrylic sealer. Allow the sealer to dry thoroughly.

Making and Adding Leaves to the Apples

1. Spray-paint one side of the wire screen with gold. Allow the spray paint to dry thoroughly. Repeat on the second side.

2. Using a pencil and the Leaf Pattern at right, trace the "leaves" onto the wire screen. You will need two leaves for each apple.

3. Using wire cutters, cut out the leaves.

4. Using a hot-glue gun and glue sticks, attach each leaf to the apple at the base of each stem. Attach two leaves to each apple.

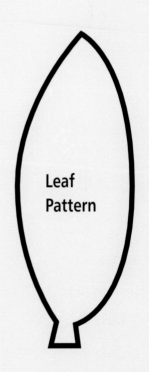

Leaf Pattern

How do I color the outside of a gourd with wax shoe polish?

Using wax shoe polish on gourds gives a warm natural effect. It is readily available, inexpensive, and easy to use. Additional coats will intensify the color.

Vessel

Here's How:

Preparing the Gourd

1. Refer to How do I clean the outside of a gourd? on page 25. Scrub the gourd.

2. Refer to Technique 1: Cutting the Gourd Open on pages 37–38. Cut only the top off the gourd. Discard the top.

3. Refer to Technique 1: Cleaning the Inside of the Gourd on pages 38–39. Clean the inside of the gourd.

4. Refer to Technique 2: Preparing the Gourd, Step 4 on page 41. Spray-paint the inside of the gourd.

Coloring the Outside of the Gourd

1. Wearing disposable gloves and using a clean rag, apply shoe polish to the outside of the gourd. Start at the bottom and work toward the top as shown at right, turning the gourd upright when the bottom is covered. Working in small circular motions, cover the entire gourd. Allow the shoe polish to dry thoroughly.

2. Using the rag, buff the outside of the gourd.

3. Repeat Steps 1 and 2 above.

Finishing the Vessel

1. Using a pencil, lightly draw designs on the vessel. Using a medium-tipped marker, color in the designs.

2. Spray the vessel with an acrylic sealer. Allow the sealer to dry thoroughly.

5
technique

What You Will Need:

- Tools and supplies, see pages 24–32
- Bottle gourd
- Spray paint, black
- Wax shoe polish, brown
- Medium-tipped permanent marker, black
- Acrylic sealer

How do I color the outside of a gourd with acrylic paint?

Using acrylic paint, along with the sponge-painting technique, adds a depth and texture to the painted gourd. This is a nice contrast to a plain painted surface. Sponge-painting with gold adds highlights to the entire area.

Sugar Bowl with Removable Star-shaped Lid

Here's How:

Preparing the Gourd

1. Refer to How do I clean the outside of a gourd? on page 25. Scrub the gourd.

2. Refer to Technique 1: Cutting the Gourd Open on pages 37–38. Using a pencil and a star stencil, trace the star on the top of the gourd as shown at right. Cut out the star-shaped lid and set it aside.

3. Refer to Technique 1: Cleaning the Inside of the Gourd on pages 38–39. Clean the inside of the gourd.

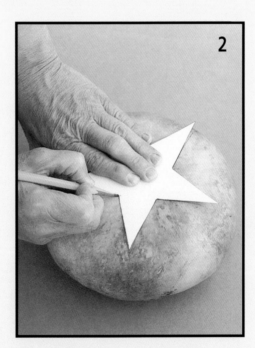

2

4. Using needle-nosed pliers, remove the stem from the lid.

Note: If a stem does not "snap off" cleanly, it must be sanded with sandpaper until smooth.

6
technique

What You Will Need:

- Tools and supplies, see pages 24–32
- Canteen or turban gourd
- Star stencil
- Acrylic paints: blue, cream, gold, red
- Medium-tipped permanent marker, black
- Acrylic sealer
- Craft knife
- Craft sticks (2)
- Leather cord, blue, 8"

Coloring the Outside of the Gourd

1. Draw a line on the gourd beginning at each point of the star to the next leg of the star, positioned 1/2" from the inside point as shown below and in Diagram A.

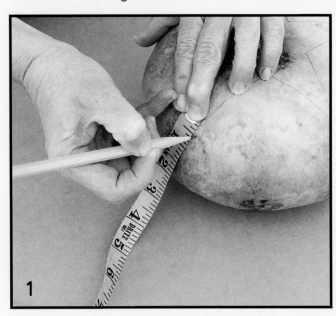

2. Mask off the drawn area with masking tape.

Note: The "white" star represents the lid that has been cut from the top of the gourd. The "black" area represents the masked-off portion.

Diagram A

3. Using a natural sea sponge, sponge-paint the area below the masking tape and the lid with red. Allow the paint to dry thoroughly.

4. Sponge-paint over the red with cream. Allow the paint to dry thoroughly. Remove the masking tape.

5. Using a soft-bristled paintbrush, paint the masked area with blue.

6. Lightly sponge-paint over the entire gourd with gold. Allow the paint to dry thoroughly.

7. Using a medium-tipped marker, outline the area painted blue at the top of the gourd.

8. Using the soft-bristled paintbrush, paint the top and edges of the lid with gold. Allow the paint to dry thoroughly.

Finishing the Bowl and Lid

1. Spray the bowl and the lid with an acrylic sealer. Allow the sealer to dry thoroughly.

2. Using a craft knife, cut 1" from each end of the craft sticks. You will be using the 1" lengths with the rounded ends to make "supports" for the lid.

Note: When you make a container with a lid, and the shape of the gourd is flat like that of a canteen gourd, there is a risk that the lid could fall into the inside of the gourd.

3. Using a hot-glue gun and glue sticks, apply hot glue to the cut end of each craft stick piece and attach it to the inside of the bowl at the outer points, making certain to leave approximately 1/2" of the rounded end exposed.

Note: The lid will rest on these supports.

4. Using a 1/8" drill bit, drill two holes approximately 1" apart at the top of the lid.

5. Push one end of the leather cord through each hole from the outside and tie a knot at each end on the inside of the lid.

How do I cover the outside of a gourd with printed tissue paper and découpage medium?

The use of paper with a white background and a small printed image works the best. Here we have used a paper that has a Victorian look, but with this découpage technique, the artist is given the opportunity to create many interesting effects. Using a printed tissue paper along with a glazing medium will produce an antique appearance.

Victorian Gourd

Here's How:

Preparing the Gourd

1. Refer to How do I clean the outside of a gourd? on page 25. Scrub the gourd.

Découpaging the Outside of the Gourd

1. Tear the tissue paper into pieces approximately 2" square.

Note: Do not cut the tissue paper as this makes the pieces too uniform.

2. In a plastic container, thin a small amount of découpage medium with water. Lay the gourd on its side and, using a china-bristle paintbrush, apply a light coat of the thinned découpage medium to a 6"-diameter area at the bottom of the gourd as shown at right.

What You Will Need:

- Tools and supplies, see pages 24–32
- Martin House gourd
- Découpage medium, matte finish
- Plastic container
- Printed tissue paper
- Glazing medium, brown
- Acrylic paint, gold
- Metallic powder, gold
- Craft wire, green, 12"
- Acrylic sealer

3. Overlapping the edges, apply the tissue paper pieces on the wet découpage medium and pat down.

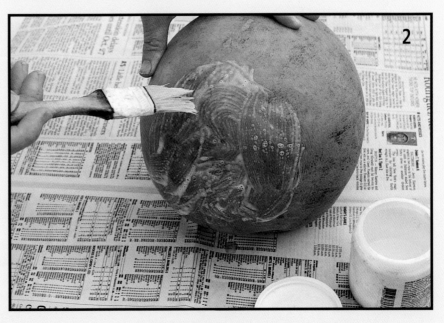

4. Using the paintbrush, apply a light coat of the thinned découpage medium over the tissue paper pieces as shown below.

5. When the découpage medium is almost dry, smooth the tissue paper down with your hand. Allow the découpage medium to dry thoroughly.

6. Continue working around and up the gourd, repeating Steps 2–3 on page 51 and Steps 4–5 above. Cover the entire gourd.

Highlighting the Outside of the Gourd

1. Using a clean rag, apply a small amount of glazing medium to the outside of the gourd. Start at the bottom and work toward the top, turning the gourd upright when the bottom is covered. Cover the entire gourd.

2. Using the rag, wipe off any excess glazing medium. Allow the glazing medium to dry thoroughly.

3. Using a soft-bristled paintbrush, apply the metallic powder to the outside of the gourd.

4. Using a clean rag, wipe off any excess metallic powder. Allow the metallic powder to dry thoroughly.

Finishing the Gourd

1. Using the soft-bristled paintbrush, paint the stem. Allow the paint to dry thoroughly.

2. Bend the length of craft wire in half and beginning at the center of the wire, wrap it around the stem approximately four times. One end at a time, wrap each wire end around a pencil and carefully slip the pencil out of the coil.

3. Spray the gourd with an acrylic sealer. Allow the sealer to dry thoroughly.

Design Tips:

• Instead of using colored wire as a finishing touch, use wired ribbon.

• Add a leaf to the top of the gourd. Use the Leaf Pattern on page 45.

• Paint the gourd, then leave a space between the pieces of paper instead of overlapping them.

How do I stitch pine needles onto the top edge of a gourd bowl with waxed linen?

8
technique

What You Will Need:

- Tools and supplies, see pages 24–32
- Bottle gourd
- Floor wax
- Pine needles
- Towel
- Waxed linen, purple
- Basketry awl
- Decorative pod
- Decorative beads (2)

Pine needles stitched around the top edge of the gourd complement its natural shape and color. Together with the seed pod, a subtle design statement can be made. Attach a few beads to add a tiny bit of sparkle.

Pine-needle-edged Bowl

Here's How:

Preparing the Gourd

1. Refer to How do I clean the outside of a gourd? on page 25. Scrub the gourd.

2. Refer to Technique 1: Cutting the Gourd Open on pages 37–38. Cut the gourd as shown in the photo on page 54. Discard the top.

3. Refer to Technique 1: Cleaning the Inside of the Gourd on pages 38–39. Clean the inside of the gourd.

Finishing the Bowl

1. Refer to Technique 1: Finishing the Bowl, Step 3 on page 39. Seal the bowl.

2. Using an electric drill with a ¹/₁₆" drill bit, drill holes parallel to the top edge, approximately ¹/₄" down and ³/₄" apart, all the way around the bowl.

3. Using sandpaper, lightly sand the inside of the bowl to smooth any rough edges around the drilled holes.

4. Soak the pine needles in warm water for approximately 30 minutes.

5. Remove the pine needles from the water and wrap them in a damp towel to keep them moist.

6. Thread a doubled 36" length of waxed linen through the eye of a needle. Knot the ends together.

7. Choose which area of the bowl will be the front. Starting there, push the threaded needle from the inside of the bowl through to the outside as shown below.

8. Lay three pine needles at a time along the top edge of the bowl and pull the threaded needle over them. Push the needle back into the inside of the bowl, and out the next hole as shown at top right. Continue until you have gone completely around the gourd.

Note: When the bunch of pine needles gets too thick—about every two inches—trim some of the earlier pine-needle ends with scissors to make them more manageable.

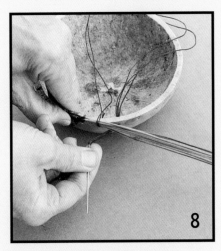

9. Using a basketry awl, tighten up the stitches by pulling the thread up and forward in the same direction as the stitching.

10. When you have gone completely around the bowl, knot the thread on the inside.

Note: Depending on the size of the opening, you may have to tie off the waxed linen and rethread the needle. It is not unusual to do this a few times.

11. Using scissors, trim the tips from the pine needles.

12. Using the ¹/₁₆" drill bit, drill a hole through the stem of the decorative pod.

13. Thread both ends of waxed linen through the pod. Slide the pod up to the pine needles and secure with a knot. Approximately 1" below the pod, tie a knot on each length of waxed linen. Add a decorative bead to each length and secure with a knot below each bead.

9
technique

What You Will Need:

- Tools and supplies, see pages 24–32
- Bottle gourds (2)
- Spray paint, white
- Acrylic paints: black, orange
- Cord, black
- Buttons, black (3)
- Doll hat
- Acrylic sealer

How do I attach one gourd on top of another gourd?

Attaching gourds together offers a unique design element when working with gourds. Limited only by the variety of the gourd, your project can take on a new dimension.

Snowman

Here's How:

Preparing the Gourds

1. Refer to How do I clean the outside of a gourd? on page 25. Scrub the gourds.

2. Refer to Technique 1: Cutting the Gourd Open on pages 37–38. Refer to photo below. Cut the bottom off the smaller gourd. Discard the bottom.

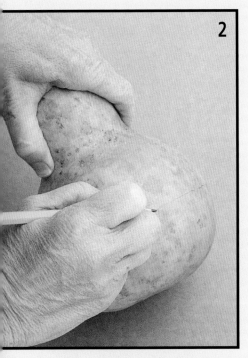

3. Refer to Technique 1: Cleaning the Inside of the Gourd on pages 38–39. Clean the inside of the cut gourd.

4. Using needle-nosed pliers, remove the stems from the tops of the gourds and set aside.

Coloring the Outside of the Gourds

1. Refer to Technique 4: Coloring the Outside of the Gourds on page 45. Spray-paint the gourds.

Stacking the Gourds

1. Using a hot-glue gun and glue sticks, apply a line of hot glue to the inside edge of the cut gourd as shown below. Immediately set it on top of the remaining gourd as shown at right. Hold in place.

Finishing the Snowman

1. Using a soft-bristled paint-brush, paint the stems for the arms with acrylic paint. Allow the paint to dry thoroughly.

2. Using an electric drill with a $1/4$" drill bit, drill one hole on each side to accommodate the arms.

3. Attach the arms, hat and buttons with hot glue.

4. Wrap the cording several times around the snowman's waist (the point where the gourds are connected). Glue in place at the back.

5. Using the soft-bristled paintbrush, paint the eyes and mouth with black and the nose with orange.

6. Spray the snowman with an acrylic sealer. Allow the sealer to dry thoroughly.

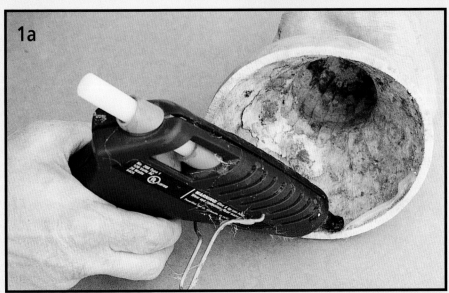

Section 3:
beyond the basics

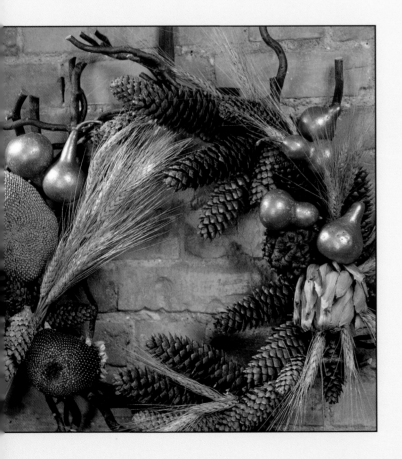

How do I make decorative eggs?

Decorative eggs crafted from gourds make wonderful year-round decorations. Brightly painted eggs, like those in this project, add a cheerful note to any room. Let the holiday determine the design—creamy pastels for Easter, "I Love You" eggs for that special Valentine, or the colors of Christmas detailed with holly leaves and berries.

Decorative Eggs

Here's How:

Preparing the Gourds

1. Refer to How do I clean the outside of a gourd? on page 25. Scrub the gourds.

Coloring the Outside of the Gourds

1. Refer to Technique 4: Coloring the Outside of the Gourds on page 45. Spray-paint one gourd with blue, one gourd with green, one gourd with purple, one gourd with teal, one gourd with yellow, and two gourds with red.

2. Using a soft-bristled paint-brush, paint a stripe, approximately ½" wide, around the center of each gourd with acrylic paints. Allow the paint to dry thoroughly.

3. Paint another stripe, approximately ¼" wide, centered on top of the previous stripe. Allow the paint to dry thoroughly.

4. Using a sponge dauber, paint a series of dots on one end of each gourd with acrylic paints. Hang them from their stems to dry. Allow the paint to dry thoroughly.

5. Repeat for the remaining ends.

6. Using the paintbrush, paint a smaller dot, centered on top of each dot. Allow the paint to dry thoroughly.

7. Using a wide-tipped marker, draw a line on each side of the painted stripes. Make a dot in the center of each painted dot.

8. Using a fine-tipped marker, draw a line around each painted dot.

Finishing the Eggs

1. Spray the eggs with an acrylic sealer. Allow the sealer to dry thoroughly.

2. Using needle-nosed pliers, remove the stems.

Note: If a stem does not "snap off" cleanly, it must be sanded with sandpaper until smooth.

1
project

What You Will Need:

- Tools and supplies, see pages 24–32
- Egg gourds (6)
- Spray paints: blue, green, purple, red, teal, yellow
- Acrylic paints: pink, dark purple, light purple, red, teal, yellow
- Fine-tipped permanent marker, metallic gold
- Wide-tipped permanent marker, metallic gold
- Acrylic sealer

How do I embellish a wreath with gourds?

Embellishing a wreath is a great way to use mini gourds. They can be left in their natural state or painted to complement any theme. This holiday wreath was sponge-painted with metallic bronze to add a touch of elegance and richness.

Wreaths for any occasion can be easily created. For a spring wreath, paint the gourds with pastel colors and add pretty ribbons. For a festive touch, add sparkle with glitter glue. Your creativity can be unlimited!

What You Will Need:

- Tools and supplies, see pages 24–32
- Mini gourds
- Dried twig wreath with selected decorative elements
- Acrylic paint, metallic bronze
- Acrylic sealer
- Craft wire

Autumn Wreath

Here's How:

Preparing the Gourds

1. Refer to How do I clean the outside of a gourd? on page 25. Scrub the gourds.

Coloring the Outside of the Gourds

1. Using a natural sea sponge, sponge-paint the gourds with metallic bronze. Allow the paint to dry thoroughly.

Finishing the Wreath

1. Spray the gourds with an acrylic sealer. Allow the sealer to dry thoroughly.

2. Using a hot-glue gun and glue sticks, randomly position and attach the gourds to the wreath.

3. Attach the craft wire to the back of the wreath and twist the ends together to form a loop for hanging.

3
project

What You Will Need:

- Tools and supplies, see pages 24–32
- Egg gourd
- Spray paint, navy blue
- Acrylic paints: black, dark blue, red, white, yellow
- Acrylic sealer
- Florist picks (4)
- Super-strength glue
- Craft wire

How do I make a critter?

The variety of cute critters that can be made from gourds is limited only by your imagination. Try the bright happy colors shown here or opt for more realistic "barnyard" animals. This is an especially fun, easy, and inexpensive craft for children of all ages. Add craft foam, felt scraps, and google eyes to help bring your creations to life.

Gourd Critter

Here's How:

Preparing the Gourd

1. Refer to How do I clean the outside of a gourd? on page 25. Scrub the gourd.

Coloring the Outside of the Gourds

1. Refer to Technique 4: Coloring the Outside of the Gourds on page 45. Spray-paint the gourd.

2. Using a soft-bristled paintbrush, paint stripes with yellow acrylic paint, approximately $1/2$" wide, from the top to the bottom of the gourd. Paint a series of dots with yellow in between each stripe. Allow the paint to dry thoroughly.

3. Paint stripes with red, approximately $1/4$" wide, centered on top of the yellow stripes. Paint a smaller dot with red, centered on top of each yellow dot. Allow the paint to dry thoroughly.

4. Paint two dots for the eyes at the top of the gourd just above the stem with white. Allow the paint to dry thoroughly.

5. Paint a smaller dot with black, centered on top of each white dot. Allow the paint to dry thoroughly.

6. Paint the stem for the nose with yellow. Allow the paint to dry thoroughly.

Finishing the Critter

1. Spray the critter with an acrylic sealer. Allow the sealer to dry thoroughly.

2. Using the soft-bristled paintbrush, paint the florist picks with dark blue. Paint the bottoms with yellow. Allow the paint to dry thoroughly.

3. Using an electric drill with a ⅛" drill bit, drill four holes into one side of the critter, approximately 2" apart in order to make the critter stable for standing. Insert the pointed ends of the florist picks into the holes. Secure in place with super-strength glue.

Note: Depending on the size of the gourd, it may be necessary to trim the ends of the florist picks as much as 1½".

4. Wrap the wire from each florist pick around the pick.

5. Drill a hole into the bottom of the critter.

6. Wrap a piece of craft wire for the tail around a pencil. Carefully slip the pencil out of the coil. Insert the coiled wire into the hole. Secure in place with super-strength glue.

How do I make a luminary?

Luminaries are wonderful additions to any outdoor evening party or barbecue. The amount of light will depend on the size and placement of the drilled holes. Try a simple cactus pattern on brightly painted gourds for a fiesta atmosphere or an airy, lacy motif on silver- or gold-leafed gourds for a romantic wedding celebration.

What You Will Need:

- Tools and supplies, see pages 24–32
- Bottle gourd
- Spray paints: black, red
- Acrylic paints: white, yellow
- Acrylic sealer
- Medium-tipped permanent marker, metallic gold
- Sand
- Votive candleholder with votive candle

Luminary

Here's How:

Preparing the Gourd

1. Refer to How do I clean the outside of a gourd? on page 25. Scrub the gourd.

2. Refer to Technique 1: Cutting the Gourd Open on pages 37–38. Cut the gourd below the neck. Discard the top.

3. Refer to Technique 1: Cleaning the Inside of the Gourd on pages 38–39. Clean the inside of the gourd.

Coloring the Outside of the Gourd

1. Refer to Technique 4: Coloring the Outside of the Gourds on page 45. Spray-paint the gourd with red.

2. Using a pencil, lightly draw flowers on the gourd.

Note: Make certain the flower design does not go too far down on the side of the gourd. Allow enough space for approximately 2" of sand to be placed in the bottom of the gourd.

3. Using a soft-bristled paintbrush, paint the flowers with acrylic paints. Allow the paint to dry thoroughly.

Finishing the Luminary

1. Using an electric drill with $1/8$", $3/32$", and $11/64$" drill bits, randomly drill various-sized holes into the gourd, positioned around the perimeter of the flowers.

2. Using sandpaper, lightly sand the inside of the gourd to smooth any rough edges around the drilled holes.

3. Refer to Technique 2: Preparing the Gourd, Step 4 on page 41. Spray-paint the inside of the gourd with black.

4. Spray the luminary with an acrylic sealer. Allow the sealer to dry thoroughly.

5. Using a medium-tipped marker, outline the drilled holes on the outside of the luminary and accentuate the flowers.

6. Place approximately 2" of sand in the bottom of the luminary. Set the votive candleholder securely in the sand.

5

project

What You Will Need:

- Tools and supplies, see pages 24–32
- Bottle gourd
- Floor wax
- Raffia
- Waxed linen, dark green
- Basketry awl
- Decorative beads

How do I embellish the top edge of a gourd bowl with raffia?

Embellishing the top edge of a gourd is a simple, yet effective way to enhance your project. Natural materials such as raffia add to the character of the bowl. Other materials such as leather, supple twigs and reeds, exquisite yarns, or fabric scraps can be substituted for the raffia in the instructions.

Raffia-wrapped Bowl

Here's How:

Preparing the Gourd

1. Refer to How do I clean the outside of a gourd? on page 25. Scrub the gourd.

2. Refer to Technique 1: Cutting the Gourd Open on pages 37–38. Cut the gourd below the neck. Discard the top.

3. Refer to Technique 1: Cleaning the Inside of the Gourd on pages 38–39. Clean the inside of the gourd.

Finishing the Bowl

1. Refer to Technique 1: Finishing the Bowl, Step 3 on page 39.

2. Using an electric drill with a $1/16$" drill bit, drill holes parallel to the top edge, approximately $1/4$" down and $1/2$" apart, all the way around the bowl.

3. Using sandpaper, lightly sand the inside of the bowl to smooth any rough edges around the drilled holes.

4. Using scissors, cut several pieces of raffia about 3" longer than the circumference of the top edge of the bowl. Coil the pieces of raffia together until it is approximately $3/4$" thick. Using the masking tape, secure the coil of raffia to the top edge of the bowl.

5. Thread a 36" length of waxed linen through the eye of a needle. Double the length and knot the ends together.

6. Choose which area of the bowl will be the front. Starting there, push the threaded needle from the inside of the bowl through to the outside. Pull the threaded needle over the coil of raffia, back into the inside of the bowl, and out the next hole. Continue until you have gone completely around the bowl, removing the masking tape as you go.

7. Using a basketry awl, tighten up the stitches by pulling the thread up and forward in the same direction as the stitching.

8. When you have gone completely around the bowl, knot the thread on the inside.

Note: Depending on the size of the opening, you may have to tie off the waxed linen and rethread the needle. It is not unusual to do this a few times.

9. Using scissors, trim the raffia.

10. Thread both ends of waxed linen through a large decorative bead. Slide the bead up to the raffia and secure with a knot. Approximately 1" below the large bead, tie a knot on each length of waxed linen. Add a smaller decorative bead to each length and secure with a knot below each bead.

6
project

What You Will Need:

- Tools and supplies, see pages 24–32
- Canteen gourd
- Spray paint, blue
- Cove molding, 1"-wide
- Balsa wood, $5/16$"-thick, 6"
- Wooden star, $1/2$"
- Wooden dowel, $1/8$"-diameter, 1"
- Twig
- Acrylic paints: assorted high-contrast colors, gold
- Craft knife
- Super-strength glue
- Acrylic sealer
- Leather cord, pink, 12"

How do I make a birdhouse?

Small birds need nesting spots and what better spot than the inside of a gourd. Knowing the sizes of bird species in your area is important because the size of opening must be large enough to accommodate the birds. Keep in mind that your birdhouse will probably last only one season.

70

Birdhouse

Here's How:

Preparing the Gourd

1. Refer to How do I clean the outside of a gourd? on page 25. Scrub the gourd.

Coloring the Outside of the Gourd

1. Refer to Technique 4: Coloring the Outside of the Gourds on page 45. Spray-paint the gourd as shown below.

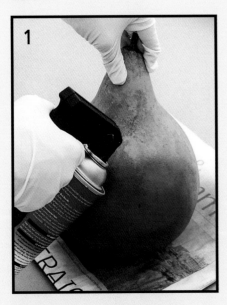

Making the Opening

1. Wearing a dust mask and using an electric drill with a 3/4" hole saw, drill a hole into the gourd as shown at right, position as desired.

2. Refer to Technique 1: Cleaning the Inside of the Gourd on pages 38–39. Clean the inside of the gourd.

Finishing the Birdhouse

1. Using a soft-bristled paintbrush, paint the cove molding, the wooden star, the balsa wood, and the twig with acrylic paints. Allow the paint to dry thoroughly.

2. Using a craft knife, cut the balsa wood into two 3"-long strips as shown in Diagram A below.

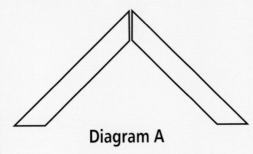

Diagram A

3. Using the electric drill with a 1/8" drill bit, drill a hole into the back of the cove molding, approximately 1/4" deep. Insert the 1/8"-diameter wooden

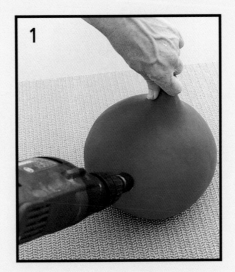

dowel into the hole for the support. Secure in place with super-strength glue.

4. Drill one 1/8"-diameter hole into the birdhouse directly above the opening. Glue the remaining end of the support into the hole.

5. Glue the balsa wood strips in place.

6. Using needle-nosed pliers, remove the stem.

Note: If a stem does not "snap off" cleanly, it must be sanded with sandpaper until smooth.

7. Using a 1/4" drill bit, drill a hole into the top of the birdhouse and a hole directly below the opening.

8. Glue the twig for the perch into the hole. Glue the star in place as shown in the photo on page 70.

9. Using the soft-bristled paintbrush, paint a circle around the perch at the birdhouse with gold.

10. Spray the birdhouse with an acrylic sealer. Allow the sealer to dry thoroughly.

11. Push the leather cord through the hole at the top of the birdhouse and out the opening. Tie a knot at the end large enough so the leather cord does not slip back through the top hole. Pull the leather cord taut and form a loop at the top for hanging.

How do I make a birdfeeder?

Watching birds eat can be an entertaining pastime. Be certain to keep the bird seed dry and the birdfeeder filled, as the birds will come to rely on the food source. Due to the elements, your birdfeeder will last only one season.

What You Will Need:

- Tools and supplies, see pages 24–32
- Martin House gourd
- Tracing paper
- Spray paint, purple
- Acrylic paints: lavender, orange, teal
- Wooden dowel, 1/4"-diameter, 18"
- Acrylic sealer
- Super-strength glue
- Leather cord, pink, 12"

Birdfeeder

Here's How:

Preparing the Gourd

1. Refer to How do I clean the outside of a gourd? on page 25. Scrub the gourd.

Making the Openings

1. Transfer the Birdfeeder Opening Pattern from page 74 onto tracing paper. Using scissors, cut out the pattern.

2. Using masking tape, adhere the pattern to one side of the gourd.

3. Using a pencil, trace the pattern as shown at right. Remove the pattern.

4. Repeat Steps 2 and 3 above on the opposite side of the gourd.

5. Refer to Technique 1: Cutting the Gourd Open on pages 37–38. Cut the openings in the gourd. Discard the pieces.

6. Refer to Technique 1: Cleaning the Inside of the Gourd on pages 38–39. Clean the inside of the gourd.

Coloring the Outside of the Gourd

1. Refer to Technique 4: Coloring the Outside of the Gourds on page 45. Spray-paint the gourd.

73

2. Using a soft-bristled paintbrush, paint the cut edge of the openings with lavender acrylic paint. Allow the paint to dry thoroughly.

3. Using a sponge dauber, paint dots around the arches of the openings with orange. Allow the paint to dry thoroughly.

4. Using the soft-bristled paintbrush, paint designs on top of the orange dots with teal. Allow the paint to dry thoroughly.

5. Paint the wooden dowel for the perch with teal. Decorate it with orange. Allow the paint to dry thoroughly.

Finishing the Birdfeeder

1. Using the electric drill with a ¹/₄" drill bit, drill a hole into the birdfeeder directly below the opening on one side. Repeat on the opposite side, aligning the holes as well as possible.

2. Insert the perch into one hole, through the birdfeeder, and out the other hole. Secure in place with super-strength glue.

3. Using needle-nosed pliers, remove the stem.

Note: If a stem does not "snap off" cleanly, it must be sanded with sandpaper until smooth.

4. Using a ⁷/₆₄" drill bit, drill a hole into the top of the birdfeeder.

5. Spray the birdfeeder with an acrylic sealer. Allow the sealer to dry thoroughly.

6. Push the leather cord through the hole at the top of the birdfeeder and out one opening. Tie a knot at the end large enough so the leather cord does not slip back through the top hole. Pull the leather cord taut and form a loop at the top for hanging.

Adjust pattern size
to accommodate gourd size

**Birdfeeder
Opening
Pattern**

How do I make a decorative container?

8
project

The Martin House gourd is perfect for making all types of containers. Containers can be created by cutting differently shaped holes in different sections of the gourd. Lids can be designed from sections of the gourd that were cut away or from other materials such as clay or tin.

What You Will Need:

- Tools and supplies, see pages 24–32
- Martin House gourd
- Plastic ring, 3"-diameter
- Coin
- Spray paint, burgundy
- Acrylic paints: black, metallic gold, teal, white, yellow
- Acrylic sealer
- Craft wire, 18-gauge
- Super-strength glue

Rooster Container

Here's How:

Preparing the Gourd

1. Refer to How do I clean the outside of a gourd? on page 25. Scrub the gourd.

2. Place a plastic ring over the neck of the gourd. Using a pencil, draw a line around the ring as shown below.

3. Using a pencil and a coin approximately 1" in diameter, trace half the coin on one end of the traced ring as shown below.

Note: This will create a place where the lid of the container will "line up" on the actual container, therefore allowing a perfect fit so the lid does not "fall" through.

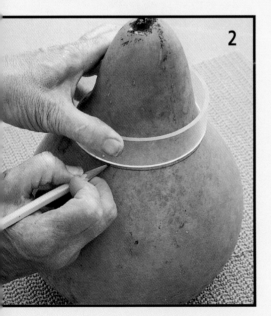

3. Paint a smaller dot with teal, centered on top of each yellow dot. Allow the paint to dry thoroughly.

4. Paint two dots for the eyes at the top of the gourd at each side of the stem with teal. Allow the paint to dry thoroughly.

5. Paint a smaller dot with white, centered on top of each eye. Allow the paint to dry thoroughly.

6. Paint a slightly smaller dot with black, centered on top of each white dot. Allow the paint to dry thoroughly.

7. Paint the stem for the nose with yellow. Allow the paint to dry thoroughly.

Finishing the Container

1. Spray the container with an acrylic sealer. Allow the sealer to dry thoroughly.

2. Bend the craft wire into a rooster's "comb." Using the soft-bristled paintbrush, paint the wire with metallic gold. Allow the paint to dry thoroughly.

3. Using an electric drill with a $^3/_{16}$" drill bit, drill two holes into the container centered vertically between the eyes, approximately 2" apart. Insert the ends of the wire into the holes. Secure in place with super-strength glue.

4. Refer to Technique 1: Cutting the Gourd Open on pages 37–38. Cut only the top off the gourd, making certain to carefully cut out the half circle.

5. Refer to Technique 1: Cleaning the Inside of the Gourd on pages 38–39. Clean the inside of the gourd.

6. Refer to Technique 2: Preparing the Gourd, Step 4 on page 41. Spray-paint the inside of the gourd.

Coloring the Outside of the Gourd

1. Refer to Technique 4: Coloring the Outside of the Gourds on page 45. Spray-paint the gourd.

2. Using a soft-bristled paint-brush, randomly paint a series of dots on the gourd with yellow acrylic paint. Allow the paint to dry thoroughly.

How do I make ladles?

The long neck and deep bowls make dipper gourds perfect for making ladles. The project here uses paints and markers to embellish the ladles for decorative purposes. However, keeping the gourd in its natural state and sealing with vegetable oil will make the ladle a useful tool in the kitchen. After serving food, clean the ladle with warm soapy water and dry thoroughly.

What You Will Need:

- Tools and supplies, see pages 24–32
- Dipper gourds (2)
- Spray paint, black
- Medium-tipped permanent marker, black
- Acrylic paints: black, white
- Acrylic sealer
- Leather cord, black

Decorative Ladles

Here's How:

Preparing the Gourds

1. Refer to How do I clean the outside of a gourd? on page 25. Scrub the gourds.

2. Refer to Technique 1: Cutting the Gourd Open on pages 37–38 and the photo below. Cut one side from each gourd. Discard the sides.

3. Refer to Technique 1: Cleaning the Inside of the Gourd on pages 38–39. Clean the inside of the gourds.

4. Refer to Technique 2: Preparing the Gourd, Step 4 on page 41. Spray-paint the inside of the gourds.

Note: If you intend to use these ladles for food, do not paint the gourds. Instead, seal them with vegetable oil.

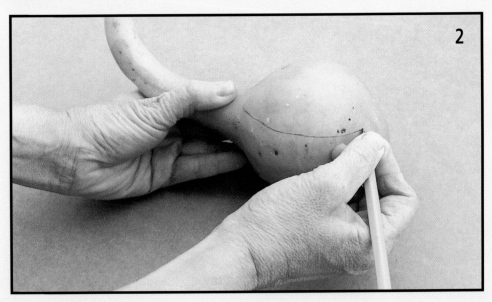

2

Adding Designs to the Outside of the Gourds

1. Using a pencil, lightly draw designs along the open edges on the gourds. Using a medium-tipped marker, color in the designs.

2. Using a soft-bristled paintbrush, paint the cut edge of the openings with black acrylic paint. Allow the paint to dry thoroughly.

3. Paint dots on top of the black designs with white acrylic paint. Allow the paint to dry thoroughly.

Finishing the Ladles

1. Using needle-nosed pliers, remove the stems.

Note: If a stem does not "snap off" cleanly, it must be sanded with sandpaper until smooth.

2. Using an electric drill with a $3/32$" drill bit, drill a hole through the neck of each gourd, approximately $1/2$" down from the ends.

3. Spray the ladles with an acrylic sealer. Allow the sealer to dry thoroughly.

4. Thread an 8" length of leather cord through one hole at the top of each ladle. Double the length and knot the ends together.

5. Embellish each ladle by wrapping leather cord around as shown at right. Using a hot-glue gun and glue sticks, secure in place.

Design Tips:

• *Instead of wrapping the neck of the gourd with black leather cord, waxed linen could be used. It comes in several colors, which allows the artist to change the color theme. Example: Change the pattern color to red and white and use red cord or waxed linen.*

• *If you keep the ends of the waxed linen exposed, beads or charms can be strung and tied onto the ends for embellishment.*

• *Try spray-painting both the inside and the outside of the gourd to change the color theme.*

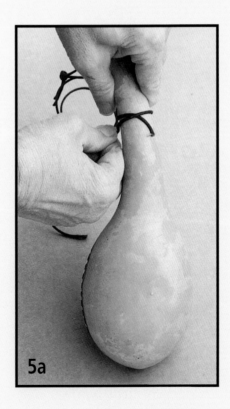

5a

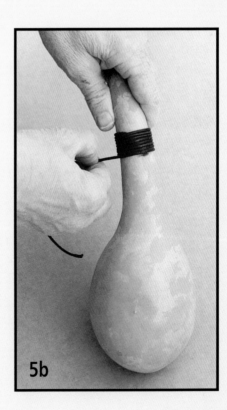

5b

10
project

What You Will Need:

- Tools and supplies, see pages 24–32
- Bottle gourd
- Spray paint, black
- Wax shoe polish, brown
- Découpage medium, matte finish
- Plastic container
- Handmade paper
- Medium-tipped permanent marker, metallic gold
- Acrylic sealer
- Leather cord, black, 12"
- Decorative bead

How do I use handmade paper to decorate the outside of a gourd?

The unique colors and textures of handmade papers can give different design finishes to gourds. In this project, a "marbled" effect was created with handmade paper. Torn pieces of paper were placed close together, but not overlapped. The result of the fine lines that appear between the paper pieces is the same as when you view the veins in marbled tile. If heavier papers are used and are overlapped, the gourd may appear to be plastered or stuccoed. Tissue-type papers, if crinkled when adhered to the gourd, may give the appearance of being wrapped with gauzy fabric.

Handmade-paper-covered Vessel

Here's How:

Preparing the Gourd

1. Refer to How do I clean the outside of a gourd? on page 25. Scrub the gourd.

2. Refer to Technique 1: Cutting the Gourd Open on pages 37–38. Cut only the top off the gourd. Discard the top.

3. Refer to Technique 1: Cleaning the Inside of the Gourd on pages 38–39. Clean the inside of the gourd.

4. Refer to Technique 2: Preparing the Gourd, Step 4 on page 41. Spray-paint the inside of the gourd.

Coloring the Outside of the Gourd

1. Refer to Technique 5: Coloring the Outside of the Gourd on page 47. Apply shoe polish to the gourd.

Découpaging the Outside of the Gourd

1. Refer to Technique 7: Découpaging the Outside of the Gourd on pages 51 and 53. However, do not overlap the paper pieces as in Technique 7. Allow areas of the polished gourd to show through, stopping at the shoulder of the gourd.

Finishing the Vessel

1. Using a medium-tipped marker, draw accent lines on the vessel, approximately ⅛" from the edge of the paper.

2. Spray the vessel with an acrylic sealer. Allow the sealer to dry thoroughly.

3. Double the length of leather cord and thread both ends through a large decorative bead creating a loop. Tie a knot at each end. Place the loop over the neck of the vessel and pull taut.

project 11

How do I make a mask?

What You Will Need:

- Tools and supplies, see pages 24–32
- Canteen gourd, minimum of 8"-diameter
- Spray paint, black
- Leather dyes: blue, brown, orange
- Wide-tipped permanent markers: black, metallic gold
- Medium-tipped permanent marker, metallic gold
- Acrylic sealer
- Leather cord, tan, 12"

When selecting a gourd for this project, choose one that is rounded on the top and bottom. If you plan on actually wearing the mask, make certain it will fit the size and contour of your face. These can also be hung on the wall in place of a framed piece or mounted on dowels and used in a masquerade or puppet show.

Owl Mask

Here's How:

Preparing the Gourd

1. Refer to How do I clean the outside of a gourd? on page 25. Scrub the gourd.

2. Refer to Technique 1: Cutting the Gourd Open on pages 37–38. Cut the gourd in half. Discard the bottom.

3. Refer to Technique 1: Cleaning the Inside of the Gourd on pages 38–39. Clean the inside of the gourd.

4. Refer to Technique 2: Preparing the Gourd, Step 4 on page 41. Spray-paint the inside of the gourd.

Making the Face

1. Using a pencil, sketch the owl face onto the gourd as shown in Diagram A at right.

Cutting the Ears

1. Using the serrated craft knife, cut the ears from the unused half of the gourd, using Diagram A as a basic pattern.

Coloring the Outside of the Gourd

1. Wearing disposable gloves and using the leather dye applicator, apply leather dye to the outside of the gourd. Color in the areas as shown in the photo on page 82. Apply leather dye to the ears.

2. Wait approximately 10 minutes, then using a clean rag, wipe off any excess dye. Allow the dye to dry thoroughly. This will take approximately two hours.

3. Using a wide-tipped black marker, outline the blue area, the eye area, and the feathers. Color the stem for the beak.

4. Using a medium-tipped metallic gold marker, outline the exterior and the interior of the ears.

5. Using a wide-tipped metallic gold marker, outline the eyes, beak, and feathers.

Finishing the Mask

1. Using an electric drill with a $7/16$" drill bit, drill two holes for the eyes.

2. Using a $1/8$" drill bit, drill one hole on each side of the mask approximately 2" down from the top.

3. Using a hot-glue gun and glue sticks, secure the ears in place.

4. Spray the mask with an acrylic sealer. Allow the sealer to dry thoroughly.

5. Push one end of the leather cord through each hole from the inside and tie a knot at each end on the outside of the mask.

Diagram A

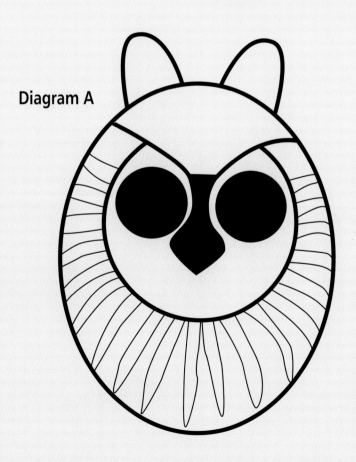

How do I make a piggy bank?

What You Will Need:

- Tools and supplies, see pages 24–32
- Bottle gourd
- Gourd scraps
- Spray paint, teal
- Wooden spheres (4)
- Acrylic paints: black, pink, white, yellow
- Acrylic sealer
- Raffia
- Cork stopper to fit opening in gourd

The challenge with a project like this is to find a cork that is the same size as the opening in the gourd. You can either find the gourd and then search for a cork to fit or find the cork and search for the gourd. If it is impossible to find one for the other, there are other solutions. You can take a cork that is too small and wrap it with embroidery floss until it is a snug fit. You could take a cork that is too big and "carve" it to fit the opening. The idea of the cork stopper can also be used to create candy jars, popcorn containers, and wine decanters.

Piggy Bank

Here's How:

Preparing the Gourd

1. Refer to How do I clean the outside of a gourd? on page 25. Scrub the gourd.

2. Refer to Technique 1: Cutting the Gourd Open on pages 37–38. Cut only the top off the gourd at the neck. Discard the top.

3. Refer to Technique 1: Cleaning the Inside of the Gourd on pages 38–39. Clean the inside of the gourd.

4. Refer to Technique 2: Preparing the Gourd, Step 4 on page 41. Spray-paint the inside of the gourd.

Making the Coin Slot

1. Using the serrated craft knife, cut a slot approximately 1¼" long and ¼" wide in the top of the gourd.

Cutting the Ears

1. Using the serrated craft knife, cut the ears from unused scraps of gourd using Diagram A on page 83 as a basic pattern.

Coloring the Outside of the Gourd

1. Using a hot-glue gun and glue sticks, secure the feet and the ears in place.

2. Refer to Technique 4: Coloring the Outside of the Gourds on page 45. Spray-paint the gourd.

3. Using a ½" sponge dauber, randomly apply dots on the gourd with pink acrylic paint. Allow the paint to dry thoroughly.

4. Using a ¼" sponge dauber, paint a smaller dot with yellow, centered on top of each pink dot. Allow the paint to dry thoroughly.

5. Using a soft-bristled paintbrush, paint two dots for the eyes at the top of the gourd just below the ears with white. Allow the paint to dry thoroughly.

6. Paint a smaller dot with black, centered on top of each eye. Allow the paint to dry thoroughly.

Finishing the Bank

1. Spray the bank with an acrylic sealer. Allow the sealer to dry thoroughly.

2. Using an electric drill with a ¼" drill bit, drill a hole into the top end of the bank.

3. Braid several strands of raffia for the tail and tie off at one end. Tightly tape the remaining end with masking tape.

4. Insert the end of the braid with the masking tape into the drilled hole. Secure in place with hot glue.

5. Insert the cork stopper into the opening in the gourd.

> **Design Tips:**
>
> • Instead of using the braided raffia tail, make a wire tail like the one for the Gourd Critter on page 64.
>
> • Use a gourd that has a very long neck to create a piggy bank with a very long nose.

13
project

What You Will Need:

- Tools and supplies, see pages 24–32
- Canteen gourd
- Circle template
- Card stock
- Spray paint, black
- Acrylic paint, black
- Wax shoe polish, brown
- Leaf stencil
- Acrylic sealer
- Upholstery tacks

How do I cut a decorative edge and stencil on a gourd?

Calculating the size and cutting the scallops on this particular project will be a challenge. A bit of practice is in order. The stenciling around the bowl adds that special touch and allows for any theme to be incorporated into the design.

Scallop-edged Bowl

Here's How:

Cleaning the Gourd

1. Refer to How do I clean the outside of a gourd? on page 25. Scrub the gourd.

Calculating the Size of the Scallops

1. Using a tape measure, measure the circumference of the gourd and find a number that will divide evenly into it.

Note: For example, if the circumference of the gourd is 48" it can be divided equally. Forty-eight divided by six equals eight, therefore eight scallops will fit around the top edge of the gourd.

2. Using a pencil and a 6"-diameter circle template, draw a circle onto card stock. Using scissors, cut out the template.

Cutting the Gourd

1. Using a pencil, draw a line around the gourd approximately ³/₄ of the way up. Find and mark the center of the circle template.

2. Place the template on the side of the gourd, lining up the line on the template with the line on the gourd.

3. Trace the curve onto the gourd. Move the template and continue tracing until the curves go completely around the gourd.

4. Draw two lines under each curve approximately ¹/₄" and ¹/₂" down.

5. Refer to Technique 1: Cutting the Gourd Open on pages 37–38. Starting at the top line under each curve, drill holes in each section. Cut the scallops. Discard the top.

Cleaning the Gourd

1. Refer to Technique 1: Cleaning the Inside of the Gourd on pages 38–39. Clean the inside of the gourd.

2. Refer to Technique 2: Preparing the Gourd, Step 4 on page 41. Spray-paint the inside of the gourd.

Coloring the Outside of the Gourd

1. Using a soft-bristled paintbrush, paint the cut edge of the gourd with black acrylic paint. Paint the decorative band along each curve with black. Allow the paint to dry thoroughly.

2. Using a leaf stencil, trace the leaves onto the gourd. Paint the leaves with black. Allow the paint to dry thoroughly.

3. Refer to Technique 5: Coloring the Outside of the Gourd on page 47. Apply shoe polish to the gourd.

Finishing the Bowl

1. Spray the bowl with an acrylic sealer. Allow the sealer to dry thoroughly.

2. Push upholstery tacks into the gourd as shown in the photo on page 86.

Note: Depending on the thickness of the gourd, you may need to cut off the tip of the tacks with wire cutters. This will keep the tacks from extending too far into the inside of the gourd.

14
project

What You Will Need:

- Tools and supplies, see pages 24–32
- Gourd scraps
- Card stock
- Acrylic paint, black
- Decorative paper
- Découpage medium, matte finish
- Plastic container
- Craft knife
- Gold leaf adhesive
- Gold leaf
- Super-strength glue
- Earring findings
- Decorative beads
- Leather cord, black

How do I make earrings and a necklace?

This is a perfect project for using up broken or less-than-perfect gourds. Gourd jewelry is as light as a feather and the design and color possibilities are endless. Gourd jewelry can be designed so that the surface of the gourd is the main element or it can be used as only a base to add additional embellishments, such as silk, brocade trims, beads, charms, etc. You will also want to remember to cover the back of the jewelry with felt, velvet, or ultrasuede to give it a more "finished" appearance.

Jewelry

Here's How:

Cutting the Earrings and the Necklace

1. Find two pieces of scrap gourd that have the same general curve to them.

2. Using a pencil, draw a template onto card stock. Using scissors, cut out the template.

Note: Keep the design shape simple.

3. Trace the template onto the gourd scraps twice—one for each earring.

4. Using a serrated craft knife, cut out the shapes. If necessary, using sandpaper, sand the edges to get the earrings as symmetrical as possible.

5. Cut out a single shape as desired for the necklace. Lightly sand to smooth any rough edges.

Painting and Découpaging the Earrings and Necklace

1. Using a soft-bristled paintbrush, paint the earrings and necklace with black.

2. Refer to Technique 7: Découpaging the Outside of the Gourd on pages 51 and 53. Extend the paper over the edges of the gourd pieces.

3. Using a craft knife, trim the excess paper from the edges.

4. Using the soft-bristled paintbrush, touch-up the edges with black.

Gold-leafing the Earrings and Necklace

1. Using a clean soft-bristled paintbrush, apply gold leaf adhesive onto the earrings and necklace. Allow the adhesive to become tacky.

2. Carefully lay the gold leaf on top of the adhesive and gently brush it down.

Note: The gold leaf will stick only where the gold leaf adhesive was applied. The excess gold leaf will brush off.

Finishing the Earrings and Necklace

1. Using super-strength glue, adhere the earring findings in place on the back of the earrings.

2. Using an electric drill with a ¹⁄₈" drill bit, drill two holes into the necklace for the leather cord.

3. Push one length of leather cord through one of the holes from the front and tie a knot at the back of the necklace. Pull the knot flush with the back, then tie another knot in the front. Tie a series of knots and decorative beads.

4. Repeat with the remaining length of leather cord on the opposite side. Knot the ends together.

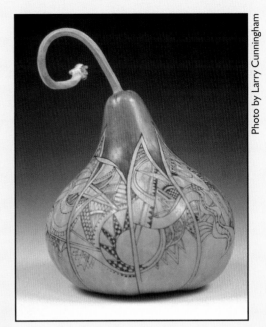

Photo by Larry Cunningham

Section 4: *gallery*

Marilynn Host

Marilynn Host was born and raised in Wisconsin. She attended the University of Wisconsin and later received her B.F.A. degree from Ohio State University. She now calls California her home where she has lived for 25 years. She lives there with her husband, Bill; the cat, Faust; the dog, Tuffy; and the parrot, Dusty.

As a mixed-media artist, Host has been working with gourds as a craft medium for 12 years. During that time she has experimented with growing gourds and manipulating the shapes into three-dimensional sculptures and vessels.

One of Host's favorite forms is animal imagery such as birds, fish, cats, and dogs. Since humor is an important aspect of Host's work, these critters often create a smile.

Host's work is represented in galleries and private collections throughout the United States.

"Gourd Birds" Dyed and airbrush-painted standing gourd birds on wood bases, with acrylic paint and wire. 6" to 31" tall x 4" to 12" in diameter.

"Gourd Baskets and Vessels" Dyed and airbrush-painted gourds with natural grapevine, waxed linen, and beads as embellishments. Approximately 8" in diameter x 18" tall.

"Gourd Vessels"
Dyed and airbrush-painted gourds embellished with waxed linen, beads, and metallic pens.
3" to 12" in diameter x 4" to 12" tall.

"Gourd Vessel and Crown of Thorns"
Dyed and airbrush-painted gourd with dyed raffia stitched and then frayed around the top.
Approximately 16"x16"x8".

94

At left:
"Giant Gourd Vessel"
Dyed and airbrush-painted
gourd with handmade cast-
paper fish handle, waxed
linen, metallic pen designs,
and clay beads. Approximately
20"x20"x20".

Below:
"Gourd Vessels"
Dyed and airbrush-painted
gourds with dyed raffia, waxed
linen, and beads. Approximately
4" to 10" in diameter x 4" to
12" tall.

Above: "Gourd Critters" Spray-painted gourds, acrylic paint, metallic wire, palm fruit stalk legs, and metallic markers. Approximately 5"x5"x5". Below: "Gourd Critters" Large gourd critter is a gourd and papier-maché, bamboo legs, acrylic paint, and metallic markers. Approximately 20"x8"x15".

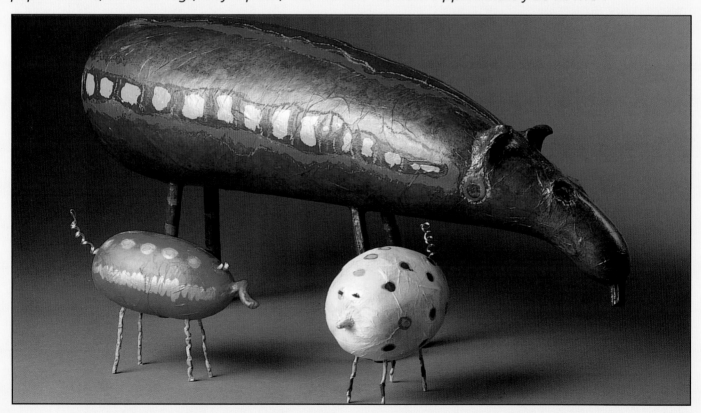

"Gourd Wall Decorations" Painted gourd and papier-maché turtle, bird, horned critter with acrylic paint, metallic markers, waxed linen, and beads. Approximately 8"x8"x10".

"Gourd Container" Dyed and airbrush-painted gourd container with handmade cast-paper fish handle, palm fruit stalks, acrylic paint, and metallic markers. Approximately 16"x16"x20".

W. Jayne Stanley

Since she was a child, W. Jayne Stanley has felt a kinship with the Earth and its inhabitants. Fulfilling her desire to preserve nature for future generations, Stanley became a forest service intern and outdoor educator, where she learned to unite people with nature. She credits her talent and spiritual connection with fibers to her grandmothers who specialized in coiled basketry for generations.

Stanley has created over 3,000 pieces that can be found in private collections and galleries around the world. She holds awards from the American Indian Art Council and numerous fine art exhibitions.

Her unique vessels, a gourd base with a coiled basket top are called "Gourdskets®." She says of her Gourdsket vessels, "Much like my children, Gourdskets have individual personalities and are named accordingly."

Photo by Azad

"The Burden Carrier" Zucca gourd stained with nature-based pigments; coiled pine needles and waxed linen embellished with leather, buffalo head nickels, tin, seed pods, and bone beads. The base was created from twined dogwood branches. Inspired by the power of ancient women's ability to carry burdens with grace and beauty. 38" tall x 16" wide.

99

"We Are Family" Apple and basketball gourds stained with multilayered nature-based pigments; coiled waxed linen and traditional western pine needles. Embellished with patined metal, clay, and glass beads. Inspired by families, which come in all shapes, colors, and varieties. 18" tall x 18" wide.

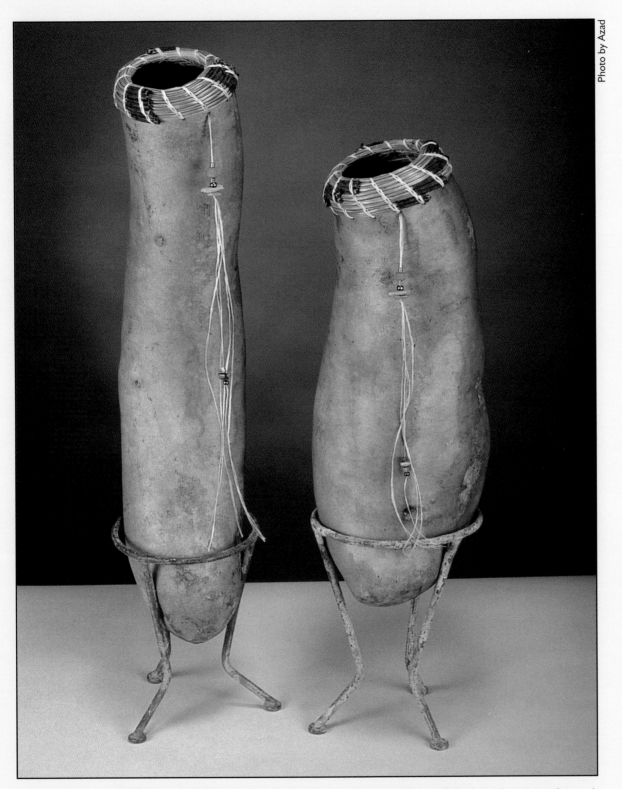

Photo by Azad

"Two Sisters—Different Fathers" Banana gourds stained with multilayered nature-based pigments; coiled pine needles and artificial sinew embellished with seeds and metal, clay, and glass beads on patined metal bases. Inspired by my daughters—their differences and similarities. 22" tall x 14" wide.

"The Drifter" Giant bushel gourd stained with nature-based pigments. Driftwood from a Colorado Rockies mountain lake. Pine needles, grasses, and weeds from the sea coiled together with waxed linen and embellished with clay, glass, and metal jewelry. Inspired by the fiber artists who drift about in search of inspiration. 19" tall x 21" wide.

Mary B. Simmons

Mary B. Simmons has been working with natural fibers most of her life, from making baskets and dolls to studying weaving and textiles while in college. Basketry became her passion. She studied with many different teachers and experimented on her own baskets.

In 1985, Simmons discovered the work of an artist who combined gourds with basket weaving. She saw the gourd as a means for artistic expression and realized the unlimited design possibilities. Simmons says, "Gourds are wonderful earthy forms, each unique and beautiful. Every gourd has a spirit of its own, and if I listen I can bring forth that essence in my work." In her creative process, Simmons gathers materials and inspiration from nature at her home in the Santa Cruz Mountains in California.

Photo by Curtis Kitchen

"Southwest Dream Keeper" Teneriffe weaving with raffia rim; philodendron sheath bead embellishment.

At left:
"Arrows Bowl"
Wood-burned arrow
design; edged with bear
grass and sisal fiber and
stitched with waxed linen
and beads.

Below:
"Southwest Bowl"
Wood-burned pottery
design; edged with bear
grass and sisal fiber and
stitched with waxed linen;
bead embellishment.

"Bamboo Bowl" Wood-burned bamboo design; edged with black bamboo twigs.

"Gourd Basket" Wood-burned geometric design; edged with banyan roots and stitched with waxed linen.

Woven gourd vessel; coiled with queen palm; embellished with fruit stalks and seed pods.

105

Sally Rosenberg

Sally Rosenberg is a native of Los Angeles, California. She received a B.A. in Theatre and Fine Arts from CSUN, and continued her studies at Penn State University.

Art has always been Rosenberg's focus, working as a set designer and graphic artist, as well as working with children's art programs. Of all the mediums she has worked with, the hard-shelled gourd is one of the most stimulating. The unique physical characteristic of each gourd influences the direction taken, often leading to unexpected, yet satisfying results. Her objective is for her artwork to complement the natural beauty of the gourd.

Rosenberg is currently exploring wood-burning and sanding techniques with the use of leather dyes.

Photo by Larry Cunningham

"Curves" Cut bottle gourd, wood-burned and left unstained. This exploration of curves is the happy result of an accidental break, which occured during the cutting process. 3" tall x 4" diameter.

At left:
"Mini Native American Pot"
Cut mini bottle gourd, wood-burned and left unstained. This piece was inspired by a combination of Native American and Art Deco influences. The design repeats three times as it wraps around, which was dictated by the gourd's shape. The polished finish is the result of sanding and buffing.
2" tall x 2$^1/4$" diameter.

Below:
"Feathers with Native American Band" Cut tobacco box gourd, wood-burned and stained. The band and feathers have been colored with leather dyes and sprayed with clear acrylic sealer.
3$^3/4$" tall x 4" diameter.

"Peeling Onion" Uncut gourd, wood-burned and stained. The decision to leave this gourd uncut was based on the rhythm and flow of the stem. The busy graphic designs are intended as juxtaposition to the simple organic elements of peeling leaves and the gourd's onion-like shape. 6" tall x 6" diameter.

"Tail Feathers" Cut bottleneck gourd, sanded, buffed, wood-burned, and stained. This repetitive, stylized design required several days just to determine the proper shape and number of feathers. Leather dye was used on the bottom half to enhance the wood-burned portion. 5" tall x 5" diameter.

Acknowledgments

I would like to thank the artists who so graciously contributed projects to be featured in the gallery section of this book.

Sally Rosenberg
15549 Devonshire Street
Suite #4
Mission Hills, CA 91345
(818) 893-7970

Mary B. Simmons
25775 Mountain Charlie Road
Los Gatos, CA 95033
(831) 438-0401

W. Jayne Stanley
GOURDSKET® VESSEL CO., INC.
P.O. Box 1413
Evergreen, CO 80437
(888) 484-7994

Special thanks to my husband Bill; my sister and brother, Karen and Bob; and all my close friends for all of their support and encouragement in this endeavor.

Many thanks to the staff at Chapelle for their patience and understanding in working with me on this project.

And many thanks to Cathy Sexton, editor, for her work in bringing all of the information together to produce this book.

Metric equivalency charts

INCHES TO MILLIMETRES AND CENTIMETRES

MM-Millimetres   CM-Centimetres

INCHES	MM	CM	INCHES	CM	INCHES	CM
$1/8$	3	0.9	9	22.9	30	76.2
$1/4$	6	0.6	10	25.4	31	78.7
$3/8$	10	1.0	11	27.9	32	81.3
$1/2$	13	1.3	12	30.5	33	83.8
$5/8$	16	1.6	13	33.0	34	86.4
$3/4$	19	1.9	14	35.6	35	88.9
$7/8$	22	2.2	15	38.1	36	91.4
1	25	2.5	16	40.6	37	94.0
$1 1/4$	32	3.2	17	43.2	38	96.5
$1 1/2$	38	3.8	18	45.7	39	99.1
$1 3/4$	44	4.4	19	48.3	40	101.6
2	51	5.1	20	50.8	41	104.1
$2 1/2$	64	6.4	21	53.3	42	106.7
3	76	7.6	22	55.9	43	109.2
$3 1/2$	89	8.9	23	58.4	44	111.8
4	102	10.2	24	61.0	45	114.3
$4 1/2$	114	11.4	25	63.5	46	116.8
5	127	12.7	26	66.0	47	119.4
6	152	15.2	27	68.6	48	121.9
7	178	17.8	28	71.1	49	124.5
8	203	20.3	29	73.7	50	127.0

YARDS TO METRES

YARDS	METRES	YARDS	METRES	YARDS	METRES	YARDS	METRES	YARDS	METRES
$1/8$	0.11	$2 1/8$	1.94	$4 1/8$	3.77	$6 1/8$	5.60	$8 1/8$	7.43
$1/4$	0.23	$2 1/4$	2.06	$4 1/4$	3.89	$6 1/4$	5.72	$8 1/4$	7.54
$3/8$	0.34	$2 3/8$	2.17	$4 3/8$	4.00	$6 3/8$	5.83	$8 3/8$	7.66
$1/2$	0.46	$2 1/2$	2.29	$4 1/2$	4.11	$6 1/2$	5.94	$8 1/2$	7.77
$5/8$	0.57	$2 5/8$	2.40	$4 5/8$	4.23	$6 5/8$	6.06	$8 5/8$	7.89
$3/4$	0.69	$2 3/4$	2.51	$4 3/4$	4.34	$6 3/4$	6.17	$8 3/4$	8.00
$7/8$	0.80	$2 7/8$	2.63	$4 7/8$	4.46	$6 7/8$	6.29	$8 7/8$	8.12
1	0.91	3	2.74	5	4.57	7	6.40	9	8.23
$1 1/8$	1.03	$3 1/8$	2.86	$5 1/8$	4.69	$7 1/8$	6.52	$9 1/8$	8.34
$1 1/4$	1.14	$3 1/4$	2.97	$5 1/4$	4.80	$7 1/4$	6.63	$9 1/4$	8.46
$1 3/8$	1.26	$3 3/8$	3.09	$5 3/8$	4.91	$7 3/8$	6.74	$9 3/8$	8.57
$1 1/2$	1.37	$3 1/2$	3.20	$5 1/2$	5.03	$7 1/2$	6.86	$9 1/2$	8.69
$1 5/8$	1.49	$3 5/8$	3.31	$5 5/8$	5.14	$7 5/8$	6.97	$9 5/8$	8.80
$1 3/4$	1.60	$3 3/4$	3.43	$5 3/4$	5.26	$7 3/4$	7.09	$9 3/4$	8.92
$1 7/8$	1.71	$3 7/8$	3.54	$5 7/8$	5.37	$7 7/8$	7.20	$9 7/8$	9.03
2	1.83	4	3.66	6	5.49	8	7.32	10	9.14

Index

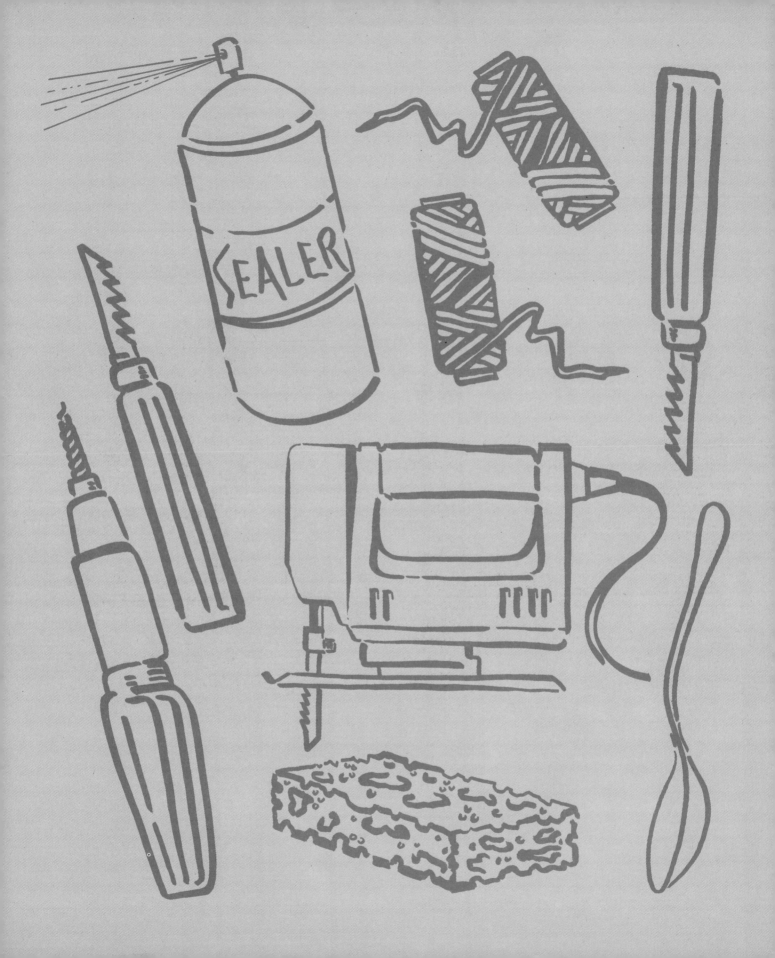